Apple Pro Training Series

Color Management
in Mac OS X

Apple Pro Training Series

Color Management in Mac OS X

Joshua Weisberg

Apple
Certified

Apple Pro Training Series: Color Management in Mac OS X
Joshua Weisberg
Copyright © 2004 by Joshua Weisberg

Published by Peachpit Press. For information on Peachpit Press books, contact:

Peachpit Press
1249 Eighth Street
Berkeley, CA 94710
(510) 524-2178
Fax: (510) 524-2221
http://www.peachpit.com
To report errors, please send a note to errata@peachpit.com
Peachpit Press is a division of Pearson Education

Apple Series Editor: Serena Herr
Editor: Anita Dennis
Production Coordinator: Laurie Stewart
Technical Editor: Tom O'Brien
Technical Reviewers: John Zimmerer, Jim Heiser
Copy Editor and Proofreader: Karen Seriguchi
Compositor: Owen Wolfson
Indexer: Caroline Parks
Cover Design: Frances Baca Design and Tolleson Design
Cover Illustration: Tolleson Design; images © Getty Images, Inc.

ISBN 0-321-24576-8
9 8 7 6 5 4 3 2 1
Printed and bound in the United States of America

To Ben and Sammy, for all the times you played trains without
Daddy while I worked on this project, and to Stacey for
your loving support and keen proofreading eye

Acknowledgments

Special thanks to Patty Montesion, John Zimmerer, and Dave Rost at Apple for their ongoing patience and assistance, and to the vendors who helped contribute to the project: Parker Plaisted from Epson, Derrick Brown and Jack Bingham from ICC, Aragorn Batsford, formerly of PhaseOne, Glen Turpin and David Allen from Quark, John Pannozzo from ColorByte Software, Liz Quinlisk from GretagMacbeth, and Steve Upton at Chromix.

To Tom Tworek, Jose Grapa, and especially my dad, Martin Weisberg: thank you for your frustration with color management, which helped me to focus on the answers. To Lee Wojnar of Group W Creative, thank you for your illustrations and the pleasure of working together again.

Of course, thanks to the folks at Peachpit Press: Karen Seriguchi and Tom O'Brien for editing, Serena Herr for making this project actually happen, and endless appreciation to Anita Dennis—thank you for your guidance, support, and encouragement.

Finally, a special note of remembrance for Carla Ow, who was always a great supporter and, more importantly, a friend.

Contents at a Glance

Table of Contents

Getting Started

Welcome to the official training course for color management in Mac OS X. This book is a step-by-step guide to setting up practical color-management workflows that actually work: It uses common graphics and layout applications and real-world scenarios. It's based on the premise that a training book should go beyond explanations of theory and software and provide you with professional techniques that you will use on a daily basis in your imaging and prepress work.

Whether you're a seasoned digital imaging and publishing professional or just getting started as a photographer or designer, you'll learn to produce consistent color you can count on. You'll learn how to set up your Mac for color management and how to move reliable color data from image capture and creation, through manipulation, and on to proofs and final output. You'll also learn how to create your own color profiles, an essential ingredient to successful color management.

The Methodology

This book emphasizes hands-on training. Each exercise is designed to help you learn how to implement color management inside and out, starting with creating profiles and configuring Adobe Photoshop, QuarkXPress, and other applications and moving on to producing final color using a full-fledged color management system. The book assumes a basic level of familiarity with the Mac OS X operating system. If you are new to color management, it would be helpful to start at the beginning and progress through each lesson in order, since each lesson builds on information learned in previous ones. If you are already familiar with the basics of color management, you can start with any section and focus on that topic.

Course Structure

This book is designed to be an introduction to color management and is not meant for those who have a great deal of experience with color management. Digital photographers, designers, and production professionals looking to implement color management will have the most to gain by reading this book.

This doesn't mean that the lessons are basic in nature. Color management is complicated, and the lessons cover some of the more detailed nuances of managing color in various applications. The book is organized into sections that reflect the ways that color management is applied at different stages of the production process:

- Lessons 1–2: Introduction to color management and ColorSync
- Lessons 3–4: Creating ICC profiles
- Lessons 5–6: Working with images
- Lesson 7: Using the Adobe Common Color Architecture and working with illustrations
- Lesson 8: Using QuarkXPress for a color-managed page layout workflow
- Lesson 9: Ensuring consistent color when printing
- Lesson 10: Color server workflows
- Lesson 11: Internet and DV color management

Introduction to Color Management and ColorSync

Lessons 1 and 2 lay the groundwork by introducing you to color management in Mac OS X and ColorSync and illustrating some of the fundamentals of color management. Lesson 2 shows you how to set up ColorSync on your computer and how to integrate ColorSync into your workflow based on which applications you use.

Creating ICC Profiles

Lessons 3 and 4 demonstrate how to create ICC profiles for different imaging devices and reviews the options for creating profiles.

Working with Images

Lessons 5 and 6 illustrate how to implement color management in Photoshop, the application in which you will probably spend most of your time while you're working with color management. Lesson 5 breaks down the complex Photoshop Color Settings dialog and demonstrates how to bring images from scanners and digital cameras into Photoshop using color management.

Lesson 6 covers soft-proofing and printing from Photoshop with color management, which are the most common color management tasks that users struggle with. These exercises will explain how to use each of the various color management functions in Photoshop. It also covers the process of saving images with color-management data for use in other applications.

Using the Adobe Common Color Architecture

Adobe has created a common color management system, called the Adobe Common Color Architecture, that is shared among the Adobe Creative Suite applications. Lesson 7 explains how the architecture works and demonstrates how to set it up. Exercises also cover how to apply color management to illustrations and designs within Adobe Illustrator.

Using QuarkXPress for a Color-Managed Page Layout Workflow

Lesson 8 reveals how to create color-managed pages in QuarkXPress, including how to create a document consisting of different color elements and how to soft-proof the document to simulate various output devices.

Printing with Color Management

Perhaps the most confusing part of working with color management is printing. There are overlapping color-management functions in applications, the operating system, and the printer software. Lesson 9 reveals the best techniques for outputting, viewing, and proofing color images, artwork, and documents, including PDF files.

Color Server Workflows

Color servers provide an alternative way to output files to color printers. Lesson 10 demonstrates how to use color management with a popular color server.

Internet and DV Color Management

Most if not all color documents are destined for the Internet. In Lesson 11, you will learn how to prepare color images and documents for accurate color reproduction on the Internet, as well as how to apply color management to digital video files.

System Requirements

This book assumes you have a working knowledge of your Macintosh computer and its operating system. You should know how to use the mouse and standard menus and commands and also how to open, save, and close files. If you need to review these techniques, see the printed or online documentation included with your system.

Basic system requirements:

- Macintosh computer with a single 500 MHz or dual 450 MHz or faster PowerPC G4 processor
- Mac OS X version 10.2.5
- QuickTime 6.1
- 384 MB of RAM (512 MB recommended)

- CD-ROM drive, required for installation of the lesson files
- 1 GB of available disk space, required for application and content installation
- Adobe Photoshop 7 or CS

Installing Trial Applications

The CD that accompanies this book includes a trial license of GretagMacbeth's ProfileMaker Pro and ColorEyes 20/20. Use the following guidelines to install these applications on your Macintosh OS X system before you begin the coursework.

1   Insert the *APTS Color Management in Mac OS X* CD into your computer's CD drive.

2   Double-click to open the Trial Software folder.

3   Double-click on the installer icon of the application you wish to install.

4   Follow the installation instructions on the screen.

Copying the Lesson Files

The CD that comes with this book includes all the media files you will need to complete the lessons. For each lesson of the book, there is a corresponding folder containing the applicable lesson files, projects, and media needed for the exercises in that lesson. On the CD, these individual lesson folders are in numeric order inside the Lessons folder. Some of the Lesson subfolders also contain additional files, such as a finished documents.

These lesson files need to be copied to your computer before you begin the coursework. When installing these files on your computer, it's important to keep all of the numbered Lesson subfolders together in the main Lessons folder on your hard drive. If you copy the Lessons folder directly from the CD to your hard drive, you should not have to reconnect your project files to the media.

Installing the Lesson Files

1   Put the *APTS Color Management in Mac OS X* CD into your computer's CD drive.

2   Create a folder on your hard drive called Color Management in Mac OS X Book Files. Drag the Lessons folder from the CD to the Color Management in Mac OS X Book Files folder.

3   Follow the instructions at the beginning of each lesson to open the project files for that lesson.

About the Apple Pro Training Series

Apple Pro Training Series: Color Management in Mac OS X is both a self-paced learning tool and the official training curriculum of the Apple Pro Training and Certification Program, developed by experts in the field and certified by Apple Computer. The series offers complete training in all Apple Pro products. The lessons are designed to let you learn at your own pace. Although each lesson provides step-by-step instructions for creating specific projects, there's room for exploration and experimentation. You can progress through the book from beginning to end, or dive right into the lessons that interest you most. Each lesson concludes with a review section summarizing what you've covered.

Apple Pro Certification Program

The Apple Pro Training and Certification Program is designed to keep you at the forefront of Apple's digital media technology while giving you a competitive edge in today's ever-changing job market. Whether you're an editor, graphic designer, sound designer, special effects artist, or teacher, these training tools are meant to help you expand your skills.

Upon completing the course material in these books, you can become a certified Apple Pro for most Apple Pro applications by taking the certification exam at an Apple Authorized Training Center. There is currently no certification for color management. Certification is offered in Final Cut Pro, DVD Studio Pro,

Shake, and Logic. Successful certification as an Apple Pro gives you official recognition of your knowledge of Apple's professional applications while allowing you to market yourself to employers and clients as a skilled, pro-level user of Apple products.

To find an Authorized Training Center near you, go to www.apple.com/software/pro/training.

For those who prefer to learn in an instructor-led setting, Apple offers training courses at Apple Authorized Training Centers worldwide. These courses, which use the Apple Pro Training Series books as their curriculum, are taught by Apple Certified Trainers and balance concepts and lectures with hands-on labs and exercises. Apple Authorized Training Centers have been carefully selected and have met Apple's highest standards in all areas, including facilities, instructors, course delivery, and infrastructure. The goal of the program is to offer Apple customers, from beginners to the most seasoned professionals, the highest-quality training experience.

Resources

Apple Pro Training Series: Color Management in Mac OS X is not intended to be a comprehensive reference manual, nor does it replace the documentation that comes with the application. For more information about color management, please refer to these resources:

- www.apple.com/macosx/features/colorsync provides an overview of ColorSync in Mac OS X.

- www.apple.com/pro/design contains a link to a white paper about ColorSync in Mac OS X.

- www.color.org is the Web site of the International Color Consortium.

- www.adobe.com/products/creativesuite/pdfs/cscolormgmt.pdf is a white paper about achieving consistent color in Adobe Creative Suite applications

- www.adobe.com/support/downloads offers ICC profiles for download.

- *Real World Color Management,* by Bruce Fraser, Chris Murphy, and Fred Bunting (Peachpit Press), is an excellent reference for color management.

1

Lesson Files   Color Management in Mac OS X Book Files > Lessons > Lesson01

Time   This lesson takes approximately 60 minutes to complete.

Goals   Learn why colors from different devices don't match

Compare the colors of different devices

Discover your devices' color capabilities

Explore the components of a color management system and see how they work together

Lesson **1**
Color-Management Basics

If I only had a dime for every time I hear, "Why don't the colors on the monitor match the colors that come out of the printer?" or "How come digital prints look different from scanned originals?" There are many reasons, based in complex color science, why the appearance of a color image is difficult to reproduce consistently on different devices. In many ways, communication in color has problems similar to those of communication in languages. Each device is like a person, speaking his or her own language. When one person who speaks French attempts to communicate with another who speaks Japanese, there is a breakdown, and the message isn't communicated accurately, if at all. Even people who speak the same language have different dialects. What's needed is an interpreter capable of interpreting the language as well as the dialect, to ensure that the message is properly communicated. The same holds true for color reproduction.

A color-management system is a system for managing color reproduction between devices, software, and the user. Much like a language interpreter, color management interprets the reproduction of color from one device to another to ensure that the intent is accurately communicated.

What You See Is *Not* What You Get

Let's do a simple exercise that will illustrate how different parts of a digital color-production workflow speak different color "languages."

1   Launch Adobe Photoshop and choose File > Open.

2   Open the sample file **Beach.tif** from the Color Management in Mac OS X Book Files > Lessons > Lesson01 folder on your hard drive.

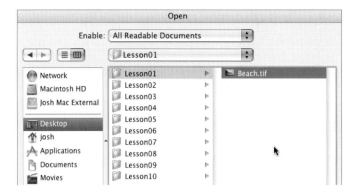

NOTE ▶ If you haven't copied the lesson files from this book's CD onto your hard drive, do so now before continuing. For instructions, see Getting Started.

3   If Photoshop displays the Missing Profile alert, select "Leave as is (don't color manage)," and then click OK. This tells Photoshop not to apply any color changes to the image.

4   Compare the image on your screen with the following image.

The image you see onscreen will typically have more contrast and more saturated colors than the image printed in the book.

5   In Photoshop, choose File > Print with Preview.

File	
New...	⌘N
Open...	⌘O
Browse...	⇧⌘O
Open Recent	▶
Edit in ImageReady	⇧⌘M
Close	⌘W
Close All	⌥⌘W
Save	⌘S
Save As...	⇧⌘S
Save a Version...	
Save for Web...	⌥⇧⌘S
Revert	F12
Place...	
Online Services...	
Import	▶
Export	▶
Automate	▶
Scripts	▶
File Info...	⌥⌘I
Versions...	
Page Setup...	⇧⌘P
Print with Preview...	⌥⌘P
Print...	⌘P
Print One Copy	⌥⇧⌘P

6   In the Print dialog that appears, check the Show More Options box and choose Color Management from the pop-up menu just below it.

7   Under Source Space, choose Document: Untagged RGB, and under Print Space, choose Same As Source from the Profile pop-up menu. We're telling Photoshop not to color manage the file but rather to send it straight to the printer.

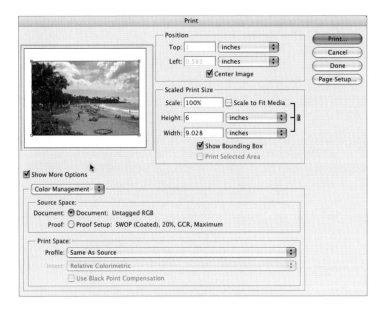

8   Click Print, and in the Printer driver dialog that appears, choose your printer from the list. My printer is the Epson Stylus Photo 2200.

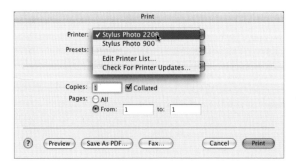

9   Click the Copies & Pages pop-up menu to locate your printer's media settings, and then choose the correct paper for your device. The location of the
media option varies with each printer; look for it under a heading such as
Print Settings. The following image shows the Epson Print Settings menu, with
Premium Glossy Photo Paper chosen from the Media Type pop-up menu.

10 Click the Copies & Pages pop-up menu again to locate your printer's
color-management options, and *turn them off*. The location of these
options varies with each printer; look for them under a heading such as
Custom, Advanced, or Color Management. The following image shows the
Color Management option in the Epson Stylus Photo 2200 printer driver,
with No Color Adjustment selected. Then click Print to start printing.

11 Compare the output from your printer to the image in the book, and to the image on your display.

The exercise you just completed does not use any color management in the process of displaying the image on your computer screen or printing the image on your printer. You probably noticed that the image onscreen doesn't match the image on the printer, and neither image looks precisely like the image printed in this book. Yet all were produced from the same digital file. This was likely not a new experience. Just about everyone who has printed a color image or document has uttered the fateful words, "It doesn't match!"

Color management systems provide color consistency and predictability across devices, reducing the guesswork and cost involved in reproducing images and artwork. Once you get color management working, you'll be able to capture, edit, and output color content with confidence. You won't be surprised by what comes out of your printer—you'll be able to predict it.

> **NOTE** ▶ The idea of *color matching* is unrealistic. It is not possible to obtain an exact match from different devices, the reasons for which will be explained a bit later. This important distinction is key in making color management work for you.

Color-Management Concepts

There are a few basic concepts to understand when working with color and color management systems. These will help you understand why color discrepancies exist and how color management works.

Device Gamut

Every color device is capable of reproducing a range of colors, better known as its *gamut*. Each device, such as a display or printer, has a unique gamut that is dictated by the characteristics of that device—the types of inks it uses to print, the type of technology it uses to capture images, and so on. Let's do another short exercise to help you visualize this concept of a color gamut.

1 Launch the ColorSync Utility that comes with Mac OS X. It is located in the Applications > Utilities folder on your hard drive.

2 Click the Profiles icon.

On the left, the utility displays a list of all of the profiles installed on your system, organized by category.

NOTE ▶ If your list of installed ColorSync profiles appears different from what's shown in the preceding image, click the downward-pointing triangle on the Profile list box and choose "Group by class."

3 Click the triangle next to Display Profiles, and select a profile for your display, such as Color LCD. Notice the location, color space, creation date, size, and other information about this profile on the right, including a 3D visual representation of its Lab Plot.

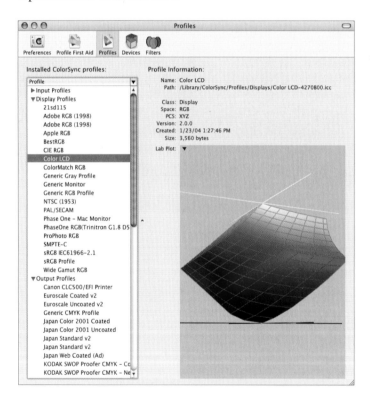

The 3D plot is a visual representation of the device gamut contained in the selected profile. The colors of the spectrum are mapped to the Lab model to illustrate the range of colors that can be reproduced.

4 Click and drag on the 3D color model to view this profile's color space from multiple angles, then release the mouse. You can also zoom in or out by holding the Option key down and dragging the mouse up and down.

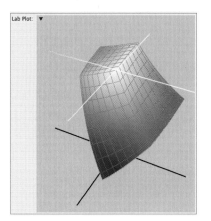 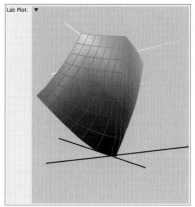

5 Click the triangle in the Lab Plot area and choose "Hold for comparison" from the pop-up menu.

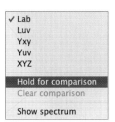

6   Now choose a SWOP press profile, listed under Output Profiles. SWOP is a common offset printing process. For example, I chose SWOP Press.

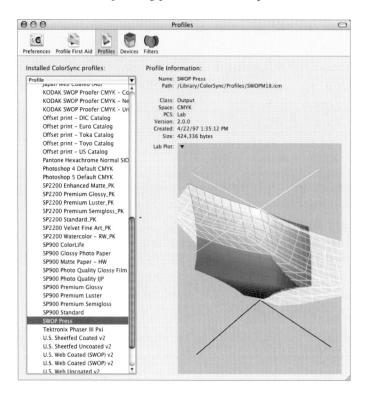

The ColorSync Utility overlays the two profiles in the 3D preview area, as shown in the preceding image, comparing the display and printer profiles we selected in this exercise. The areas in white are colors that can be reproduced by the RGB device represented by the display profile, but not by the SWOP profile (which is CMYK process color, in this case). The magenta, green, and blue colors on the plot that exceed the white area can be reproduced by the SWOP Press profile, but they will not be displayed because they are outside the color gamut of the Color LCD device in this example.

7   Rotate the overlapping color models to see their entire shapes.

Each device has a unique gamut. When the gamuts of two devices don't overlap, the colors can't be reproduced consistently across the devices. It's as if they spoke different languages. Even devices of the same type (say, two color printers) may have different gamuts—or language dialects. The colors seen on a display are typically much brighter and more saturated than the color that comes out of a printer. The reason for this is that the color on a display is in gamut for the display, but is not in gamut for the printer. The printer simply cannot reproduce all of the colors contained in the image. In this case, the color is said to be *device dependent*—whether the desired color is produced depends on the capabilities of a particular device.

Color Spaces

The gamuts of desktop devices, such as displays and printers, are relatively small when compared with the visible spectrum of light. Color scientists use mathematical models that represent color in different ways. For the purposes of color management, models that represent the visible spectrum are used, as they easily contain all of the colors that an imaging device can capture or reproduce.

These are color spaces where the definition of a color is not dependent on any particular device—they are said to be *device independent*. In 1931, the CIE (Commission Internationale de l'Eclairage) established standards for a series of color spaces that represented the visible spectrum—60 years before the arrival of desktop color! The CIE color spaces form the foundation of device-independent color for color management. Many of these spaces, such as CIE XYZ and CIE Lab, are widely used in color-management systems today.

1   In the ColorSync Utility, click again on the triangle in the Lab Plot area. This time, choose "Show spectrum" from the pop-up menu.

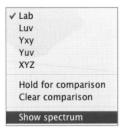

The ColorSync Utility displays the CIE Lab color spectrum around the gamut comparison.

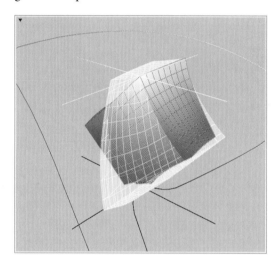

2 Rotate the model to see all sides. Device-independent color spaces, such as CIE Lab, are much larger than the gamut of the typical digital imaging peripheral. In other words, your monitor and printer can reproduce only part of the visible spectrum of light.

3 Click on the triangle in the Lab Plot area again, and select a different color space, such Yxy.

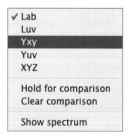

The gamut comparison of the two devices is now displayed within the CIE Yxy space.

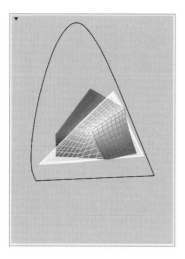

Each CIE color space has a unique shape, but they are all larger than the gamut of any individual imaging peripheral.

4 Click the triangle again and choose "Clear comparison."

Device-independent color spaces are used by color management systems in the process of transforming data from one device to another. Color from one device is mapped from the device-specific value to a device-independent value in a color space. Once in an independent space, the color can be mapped to another device-specific space.

Device Profiles

Profiles are basically dictionaries that contain data on a specific device's color information, including its gamut, color space, colorants, and modes of operation. In other words, profiles contain all the unique color characteristics of a device—and are essential to making the whole system work. Color management systems use profiles to translate color data from one device-dependent color space, such as a scanner, to another device-dependent color space, such as a printer, via device-independent color spaces. The process of creating profiles is known as *device characterization*. Device characterization is typically performed with highly sensitive color-measurement devices. We'll learn how to create profiles in Lessons 3 and 4.

Early color management systems used proprietary profile formats, which weren't compatible with each other. Fortunately, the International Color Consortium was founded to establish color-management standards, the first of which was the ICC profile. ICC profiles are based on a well-defined, open standard and are now supported by virtually all vendors of color-imaging hardware and software, as well as platform vendors like Apple and Microsoft.

ICC profiles come in different flavors, or classes:

- Input profiles support scanners and cameras.
- Display profiles support both CRTs and LCDs, and projectors.
- Output profiles support RGB and CMYK printers and printing processes.
- Color-space profiles support device-independent color spaces, such as CIE Lab.

The ICC profile specification supports other profile classes such as the ones described below; however, they are not widely used.

- Device-link profiles link two devices together directly, bypassing the device-independent color space during transformation. These profiles are essentially two device profiles in one file.
- Abstract profiles essentially manipulate the color of images. For example, the abstract profile Sepia Tone will convert an image from one device space into a sepia-toned image. Few profile-creation tools support abstract profiles.
- Name profiles express named color systems, such as Pantone, in a device-independent way. The name profile contains transformations from device-independent spaces into the specific values for the vendor's inks.

The ColorSync Utility provides a catalog of profiles installed on your system and can display them by class.

1 In the ColorSync Utility, click the Profiles icon, click the triangle at the top right of the Profile display list, and confirm that "Group by class" is selected.

2 Expand the Input Profiles, Display Profiles, and Output Profiles classes by clicking the triangles next to their names, and then successively click some profiles in each class to see their gamuts on the right side of the window.

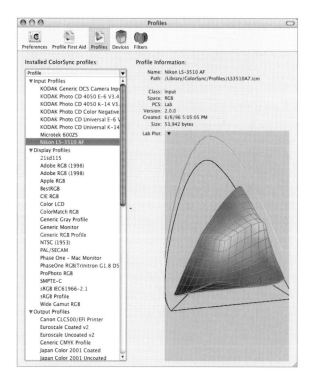

3 Click the triangle in the Lab Plot area and choose "Show spectrum" to see how each profile compares to the selected device-independent color space.

4 Expand the Colorspace Profiles section, and choose Generic XYZ Profile.

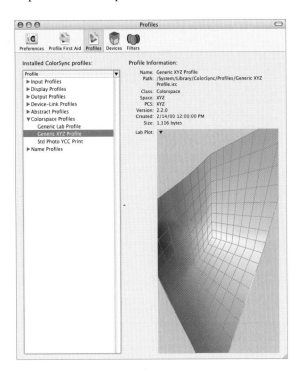

Notice how much larger the color-space profile is than a device profile.

Color Matching Method

The CMM—or color matching method, or color-management module—is the color engine that performs the transformations of color data between different profiles. ColorSync includes a CMM built by Apple, and you'll also find that some applications come with their own CMM. For example, all Adobe applications ship with the Adobe Color Engine (ACE), but they let you choose between ACE and ColorSync's CMM. ColorSync includes a System Preference for selecting which CMM is used by default.

1 In the ColorSync Utility, click the Preferences button, and then click the
CMMs button.

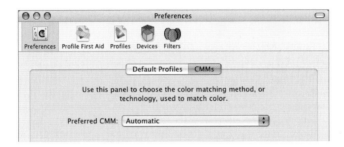

2 Choose Apple CMM from the Preferred CMM pop-up menu.

If additional CMMs are installed on your Mac, they may appear in this list.
The Automatic selection instructs ColorSync to use whichever CMM is
called for by a profile. Explicitly selecting a CMM instructs ColorSync to
use that CMM regardless of what the profile states. The Apple CMM is
included as part of ColorSync with Mac OS X.

NOTE ▸ Third-party CMMs are not always registered with ColorSync
and may not appear in ColorSync's preferences. For example, the CMM
that ships with Adobe's design applications, Adobe ACE, does not appear
on the list. This CMM can only be selected within the Adobe applications'
color-settings preference.

3 Quit ColorSync Utility.

Gamut Checks

A color-management system uses device profiles and a color matching method
to transform color data between devices to ensure accurate reproduction.
Specifically, the CMM translates data from one device's colors to another via a
device-independent color space: The CMM receives the necessary information

from the relevant profiles so that it can accurately transform a color from one device to another, producing color that is predictable from device to device. Remember, it is not possible to achieve perfect color matches between all devices due to inherent differences in each device's color gamut.

But what happens when a color is out of gamut? What if, for example, you want to print a photograph that contains colors your printer can't produce? Without color management, you'd have no way of predicting or controlling what happens to those colors, or of even knowing that they were out of gamut.

The first challenge is to determine that a color is out of gamut. The hard way is to print an image, and wonder why that bright blue color on your monitor prints like muddy blue from your printer. The easier way is to use a neat feature of color management called the *gamut check,* or as Adobe calls it, the Gamut Warning. This feature applies a device profile to an image and shows you if certain colors can't be reproduced.

1   Launch Adobe Photoshop and choose File > Open.

2   Navigate to the **Venice.tif** in Color Management in Mac OS X Book Files > Lessons > Lesson01 folder on your hard drive, and click Open.

3   If Photoshop displays the Missing Profile alert, select "Use the embedded profile (instead of the working space)," and then click OK. This tells Photoshop not to apply any color changes to the image.

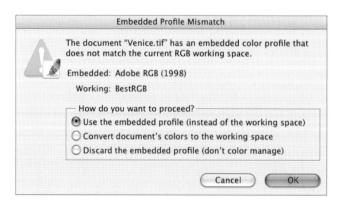

4   Choose View > Gamut Warning.

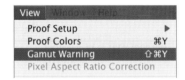

Photoshop displays the image with the Gamut Warning.

The areas shaded in gray—in the flowers in the foreground—are colors that cannot be reproduced by the output device.

5   Toggle the Gamut Warning on and off to see the affected colors (press Shift-Command-Y).

When a color is in gamut for one device but not another, the CMM must select the next closest reproducible color. This is called *gamut mapping*.

Because the use of color data varies, the intended use of a color must be specified to produce the best possible results. The ICC profile specification supports four gamut-mapping options, called *rendering intents*. Fortunately, each profile includes a default rendering intent, so if you're not sure which one to pick, ColorSync will use the default.

Rendering Intents

The ICC profile specification supports four rendering intents used to map out-of-gamut colors:

- *Perceptual rendering* works to preserve the visual relationship between colors so that they are perceived as natural to the human eye, even if the colors themselves actually change. This rendering intent is suitable for photographic images.

- *Saturation rendering* tries to produce vivid colors and sometimes sacrifices color accuracy to do so. As a result, this rendering intent is suitable for business graphs or charts in which bright, saturated colors are more important than the exact relationship between colors.

- *Relative colorimetric rendering* compares the white point of the source color space to that of the destination color space and shifts out-of-gamut colors to the closest reproducible color in the destination color space. Relative colorimetric rendering maps whites to the target output space and preserves more of the original colors in an image than the Perceptual rendering intent.

- *Absolute colorimetric rendering* leaves colors that fall inside the destination gamut unchanged, and it effectively clips colors that fall out of that gamut. This rendering is based on the source's white point and is suitable for proofing to simulate the output of a particular device.

Color Management System Interfaces

Color management systems such as ColorSync include an interface that allows software developers to utilize and manage the color-management capabilities of the system. These interfaces, known as *application programming interfaces,* or *APIs,* contain code that can be used as part of another application.

How Does It All Work?

Let's go back to the metaphor we started with at the beginning of this lesson, in which we said communicating in color is a bit like communicating in multiple languages. Color management systems act as the interpreter. The profile is like the dictionary for a device's language and dialect. Profiles are used by the CMM, which translates data from one device's colors to another, via a device-independent color space. The CMM receives the necessary information about a device from the profiles and uses rendering intents to perform gamut mapping to produce color that is predictable from device to device. The API provides access to all of these functions to applications. Remember, it is not possible to have perfect color matches between devices due to differences in each device's gamut.

What You've Learned

- Each device has a unique set of colors, or a gamut, that it can reproduce.
- Colors cannot always be matched between devices due to the differences in gamut.
- Device profiles represent a device's color-reproduction capabilities.
- A color matching method, sometimes also called a color-management module, or CMM, is the engine that transforms color between device-specific color spaces.
- Color management systems use profiles and CMMs to map color between devices to ensure the greatest possible accuracy and predictability.

2

Lesson Files Color Management in Mac OS X Book Files > Lessons > Lesson02

Time This lesson takes approximately 60 minutes to complete.

Goals Set up ColorSync preferences on your computer

Find out which profiles are used for each of your devices

Integrate ColorSync into your workflow

Determine whether an application implements its own color management

Using Color Management in Mac OS X

Color management is truly effective when it is pervasive throughout the tools you use. When color management is a core component of the operating system, it is available in a consistent manner to all of the devices and applications used in your workflow. By building color management into the operating system, Apple is enabling accurate color to be maintained throughout the imaging and publishing process.

Mac OS X contains a comprehensive color management system called ColorSync, which has been part of the Mac operating system for about 10 years. In past versions of the Mac OS, ColorSync was only accessible from within an application that supported it—there was no way for creative professionals to take advantage of its functionality unless the applications they used were written to specifically include support for ColorSync. In Mac OS X, ColorSync is thoroughly integrated with the entire operating system.

Exploring ColorSync

Most of ColorSync is transparent, working behind the scenes automatically. So where is ColorSync, and how does it work? ColorSync has an effect on color within several key components of Mac OS X:

- The Mac OS X 2D drawing architecture, known as Quartz, is the graphics-rendering system that displays text and graphics on the screen. ColorSync ensures that Quartz renders color data accurately.

- The Image Capture architecture moves data from scanners and cameras to your Mac. ColorSync automatically tags this data with the appropriate ICC profile.

- The display architecture manages displays connected to your computer. It uses ColorSync to match color data from its source to the display.

- The printing system calls on ColorSync to match color data from the display to a printer, using profiles for each device.

- The ColorSync Preferences enable you to set default profiles for each device and to manage profiles.

- The ColorSync Utility can be used to assign profiles to devices and to validate or repair profiles. The most direct interaction you will have with ColorSync is through the ColorSync Utility.

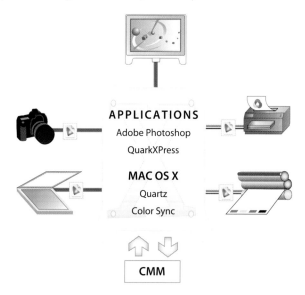

These components all function together to create a color-managed workflow, or a process of moving color data from capture and creation to manipulation and then to output, all with consistency and predictability.

Setting up ColorSync Preferences

Let's begin by setting the ColorSync preferences. This ensures that ColorSync is set up for your workflow and for the lessons in the book.

1 Double-click the ColorSync Utility filename inside the Applications > Utilities folder on your hard drive to launch it.

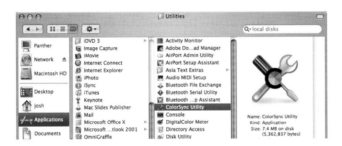

The ColorSync Utility is a centralized application for setting preferences, viewing all installed profiles, assigning profiles to devices, and repairing profiles that do not conform to the ICC specification.

2 Click the Preferences button. This is where we will determine how ColorSync will deal with different types of color data.

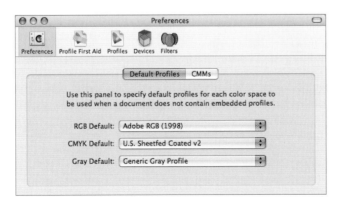

Ideally, all images and color documents will contain embedded profiles that represent the source of the color data contained within. The Default Profiles panel is where you can set a default profile for documents that do not contain embedded color profiles. You will probably come across images and documents that lack embedded data. These are known as *untagged* images or documents. The choices you make in the Default Profiles preferences will suggest to applications that explicitly support these preferences how to handle such documents based on their color space. Be aware that these settings work only with applications that explicitly support ColorSync.

NOTE ▶ In Lesson 6 you will learn how to embed profiles in untagged images.

3   Click and hold the RGB Default pop-up menu, which displays a list of profiles for RGB devices.

The RGB Default setting will suggest what profile the application should use to handle untagged RGB data. The best choice is to select either a working-space profile, such as Adobe RGB (1998), or your display profile. Either of these options will provide a good generic choice for color data that lacks a profile.

NOTE ▶ If you are working with image data that lacks an embedded profile but you know the source, you can manually tag the image with a profile. This will be covered in more detail in Lesson 6.

4 Choose Adobe RGB (1998).

5 Click and hold the CMYK Default pop-up menu, which displays a list of profiles for CMYK devices.

Typically, any CMYK data you receive will be from a high-end scanner or will already be separated for a press.

6 For the CMYK Default setting, select a profile that is representative of the likely source of the data, such as SWOP Press.

NOTE ▶ If CMYK data is not part of your workflow, leave the preference set to Generic CMYK Profile.

7 If you work with grayscale images and you have a grayscale profile, select it under the Gray Default pop-up menu. Otherwise, leave the menu set to Generic Gray Profile.

8 Click the CMMs tab.

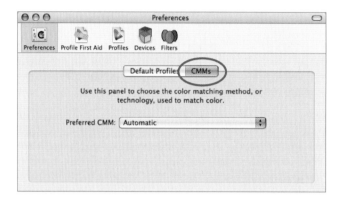

This panel allows you to choose the CMM, or color matching method, for your workflow. The CMM is essentially a mathematical algorithm that transforms your color data. In addition to the default CMM provided by Apple, several companies have created their own CMMs that are installed by their applications.

9 Under Preferred CMM, choose Apple CMM.

The Automatic option will use the CMM specified in the source profile. Selecting the Apple CMM tells ColorSync to always use the Apple CMM. Some applications, such as Adobe Photoshop, may offer the capability to override this choice. Although the results from different CMMs are typically subtle, using the same CMM will reduce any variability that might occur.

NOTE ▶ Sometimes an application, such as Adobe Photoshop, provides a similar setting within the application, and ignores this CMM preference. In that case, select Apple CMM if it is available.

10 Click the Devices button.

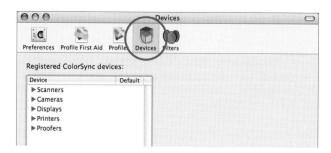

11 Expand the Displays selection by clicking the triangle to the left of Displays.

12 Choose your display, such as Color LCD, as shown in the following figure.

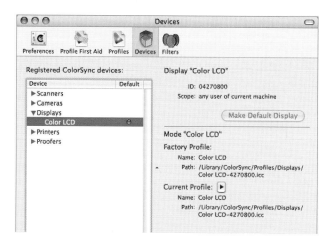

The Devices panel lists all color devices attached to the system. When you select a device from the list, it displays the profile information for that device, including Factory Profile, which is the profile that came with the device, and Current Profile, which is the profile currently in use.

The Current Profile will be the same as the Factory Profile unless changed by a user or an application. Certain applications, such as display calibrators, will change the Current Profile setting to a profile created as a result of calibration.

If the device doesn't include a profile, ColorSync will assign a generic profile when the device is installed.

13 Click the triangle next to Printers, and choose your printer from the list.

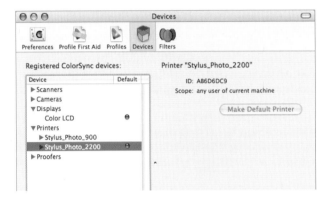

Notice that the chosen printer, the Epson Stylus Photo 2200, has a disclosure triangle. This is because it has several profiles.

14 If available, click the disclosure triangle next to the selected printer to display a list of its profiles.

The ColorSync Utility displays a list of profiles for this device. In the case of my Epson Stylus Photo 2200, the device shipped with several profiles for different papers. When a paper type is selected in the Print dialog, ColorSync automatically selects the corresponding profile if it's available. The blue dot indicates the default profile, in this case for SP2200 Standard_PK paper.

On the right side of the window, notice the triangle next to Current Profile. This allows a different profile to be selected for a device (or for a subset of the device, such as media type). If you create a custom profile, you can use this setting to change the default profile to the newly created profile.

NOTE ▶ You will learn how to create custom profiles in Lesson 4.

15 Click the Profiles button at the top of the ColorSync Utility.

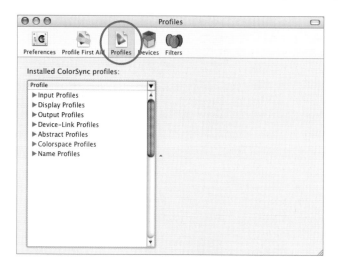

NOTE ▶ If your list of installed ColorSync profiles appears different from what's shown in the preceding image, click the downward-pointing triangle on the Profile list box and choose "Group by class."

The Profiles section of the ColorSync Utility displays all of the profiles installed on your Mac, according to profile class.

Profiles can be stored on your Mac in several folders, including:

▶   System > Library > ColorSync > Profiles — This directory contains system profiles provided by Apple. Profiles in this directory are available to all users. An authenticated user can add profiles to this directory; however, it is best to store them in the following directory, as this one is set aside for Apple.

▶   Library > ColorSync > Profiles — Profiles in this directory are available to all users, and it is the preferred location for profiles when they're added to your system.

▶   Users > *username* > Library > ColorSync > Profiles — Only the current authenticated user can use, add, or remove profiles in this directory. Store profiles here if you do not want other users of the system to have access to your profiles.

16 Click the disclosure triangle next to Output Profiles, and choose a profile from the list, such as SWOP Press.

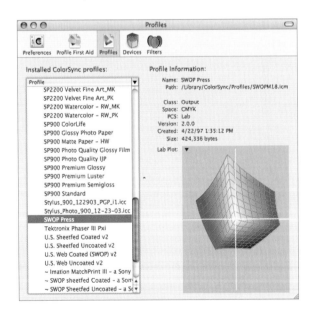

Details about the profile and a 3D rendering of its color gamut are displayed on the right of the window.

17 Move your cursor over the color model, click and hold the mouse button, and drag slowly to rotate. You can zoom into or out of the color model by pressing the Option key and moving the mouse up and down.

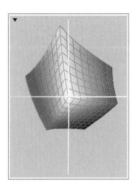 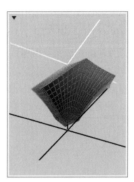

Rotating the model will show you the profile's entire color gamut, with the color of each section overlaid on the model. In Lessons 3 and 4, we will use this feature to compare profiles.

TIP Select different types of profiles and notice the shapes and sizes of the gamuts.

18 Click the Profile First Aid button at the top of the ColorSync Utility.

The ColorSync Utility's Profile First Aid feature can check the profiles on your system to ensure that they conform to the current ICC profile specification.

19 Click the Verify button. The ColorSync Utility begins scanning your profiles.

20 When Profile First Aid finishes checking your profiles, it displays a list of errors. Click Repair to fix the errors.

In certain cases, the ColorSync Utility will not be able to repair all of the corrupted profiles. This does not always mean that the profiles are useless, but simply that they do not conform to the current ICC specification.

21 Press Command-Q to close the ColorSync Utility.

22 Open the Mac OS System Preferences and click the Displays icon.

23 Click the Color tab.

The Color section of the Displays preferences allows you to select a profile for your display. You will use this profile to color match data to your display.

24 Check the "Show profiles for this display only" box. This tells ColorSync to show only the profiles that are specifically for your display.

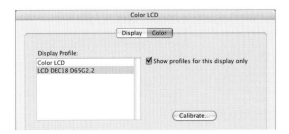

ColorSync receives information from the display and uses it to create a rudimentary display profile. A generic profile is then created for the display and selected as the default. Unless you have created additional profiles for your display, it is likely that only one profile will be listed in the Display Profile section of the Displays preferences.

NOTE ▶ Lesson 4 includes exercises for calibrating your display.

These settings we have just covered control the device profiles that ColorSync uses in your workflow. You should typically need to set these only once, unless you're adding additional devices to your system or changing a variable, such as using a new type of ink or paper.

Using ColorSync in Your Workflow

ColorSync functions at two levels: automatically at the system level, and in more complex ways with professional design and imaging applications. Let's look at how you can incorporate it into your workflow at those two levels.

ColorSync at the System Level

In the ideal workflow, color management is implemented automatically at the system level. The operating system handles everything: Device profiles are installed when a device is connected to the computer, and color data is matched from input devices to the display for viewing, and matched to printers for proofing or outputting hard copy. All color data is tagged throughout the entire workflow, ensuring that it can be moved between applications and systems without loss of information.

And with ColorSync in Mac OS X, this actually works. Let's see how.

> **NOTE ▶** Before beginning this exercise, make sure you have a digital camera, as well as a printer, connected to your Mac.

1   Double-click the ColorSync Utility icon, located in the Applications > Utilities folder on your hard drive, to launch it.

2   Click the Devices icon and choose an input device, such as the Canon PowerShot G2 camera shown in the following figure, from the list.

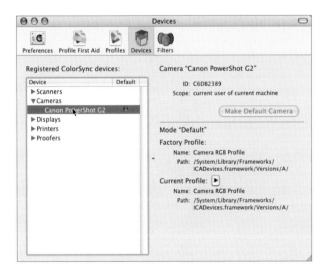

ColorSync has automatically assigned a profile for this device. If the camera driver (or scanner driver, if you chose a scanner) doesn't include a profile, a generic one is assigned, as you should see on the right side of the Devices window.

NOTE ▶ iPhoto uses ColorSync to color match images to the display, using the camera profile as a source and the display profile as the destination.

3 Leaving ColorSync open in the background, navigate to the Finder and launch Preview, located in the Applications folder on your hard drive.

4 Press Command-O to open the sample file **Beach.tif** from the Color Management in Mac OS X Book Files > Lessons > Lesson02 folder on your hard drive.

ColorSync-aware applications such as Preview recognize profiles embedded within images and documents and automatically color match them to the display, using the display profile. This ensures that they are accurately reproduced when moved from computer to computer.

5   Choose Tools > Get Info.

The Document Info window opens.

6   Notice the information for Embedded ICC Profile: Adobe RGB (1998). This profile is embedded in the sample image.

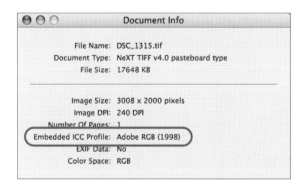

When the image is opened in Preview, ColorSync performs a color match from Adobe RGB (1998), the source profile embedded in the image, to the display profile.

You can change the default profile for the device, substituting a custom profile or using different profiles for different workflows.

7   Return to the ColorSync Utility, click the Devices icon, and choose your
     printer (and any of its associated profiles) from the list.

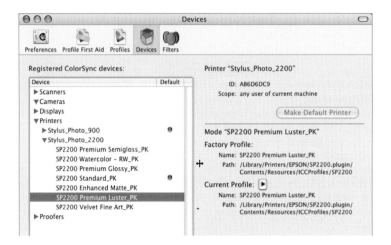

When you connect a printer to your Mac, ColorSync automatically assigns
a profile to it. If the printer driver has no profile, ColorSync assigns a generic
profile. In the case of my Epson Stylus 2200, the Epson driver contains
several profiles for different media types, as noted in the previous exercise.

8   Return to Preview, where **Beach.tif** should still be open, and choose
     File > Print.

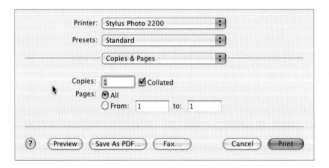

When you print, ColorSync manages the color between the source profile
and the printer profile.

9 Click the Preview button and check the Soft Proof box.

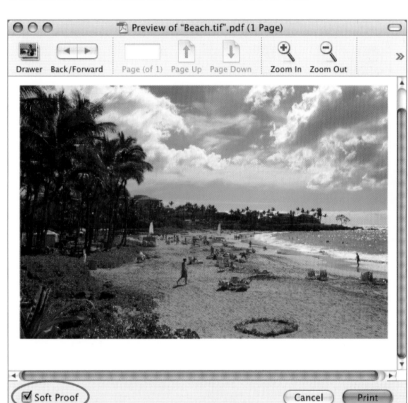

The Print Preview feature in Mac OS X uses ColorSync to perform a *soft proof,* or an onscreen simulation of the printed output. This feature uses the source, display, and printer profiles; ColorSync first matches the data from source to destination, and then to the display profile to simulate onscreen the colors of the printed output. When used properly, soft-proofing can save time and money: you can evaluate what an image will look like when printed, without printing it!

NOTE ▸ Soft-proofing images will be covered in greater detail in Lesson 6.

When you toggle the Soft Proof setting, ColorSync turns the printer simulation on and off. In some cases, the differences may be subtle, especially if the source profile and display profile have similar gamuts. With the **Beach.tif** image, the difference will be most noticeable in the sky and in the green bushes.

10 Press Command-Q to quit Preview.

ColorSync's automated, system-level approach to color management is good for consumers and others who use, for example, a digital camera, iPhoto, and an inkjet photo printer, and who don't want to think about color management— they just want colors to look right. If, however, you're a graphic designer or publisher using higher-end applications and devices to create professional four-color output, you probably want more control over your workflow.

The built-in capabilities may need to be extended using third-party utilities and applications that are appropriate for professional graphic designers and publishers.

First, applications must be ColorSync aware. Apple provides a number of ColorSync-aware applications—including iPhoto, iMovie, Mail, Safari, Keynote, and Image Capture—and numerous third-party applications also support ColorSync. The problem is that popular high-end design applications, such as the components of the Adobe Creative Suite (namely, Adobe Photoshop, Illustrator, InDesign, GoLive, and Acrobat) and QuarkXPress, do not make full use of ColorSync. Rather, companies such as Adobe have built their own color-management technologies into their applications so that they have a system that works both on the Mac OS and in Microsoft Windows and that provides more-advanced features for controlling the color workflow. As a result, the color-management technologies in these applications function apart from Apple's system-level solution.

Second, in order for an automated ColorSync workflow to work completely, support must be built into peripheral devices such as scanners and printers. In other words, scanner and camera manufacturers need to support Image Capture and iPhoto, for example, in order to have ColorSync automatically handle color management, while printer manufacturers need to support Quartz-based printing. Unfortunately, however, most professional devices ship with their own software, which includes their own form of color management. For example, higher-end scanners and cameras often include software to interface with the device and manage the capture process. ColorSync may assign profiles to these devices, but the device software will usually not use them.

Along these lines, if you are printing to an Adobe PostScript device, PostScript does not use the Quartz engine for printing. Professional applications such as QuarkXPress and Adobe InDesign usually have their own capabilities and override or prevail over system-level color management, and you will have to learn how to use them. We will cover those tools in Lessons 7 and 8. And if you send documents to a four-color offset or press, you will typically use the color-management capabilities within an application such as QuarkXPress or Adobe InDesign, as they provide more control over the color-separation process than Quartz.

Finally, ColorSync currently does not support RAW digital-camera images. Many digital cameras support a file format that contains unmodified data captured by the camera's sensor, known as a RAW file. RAW files are processed on your computer, unlike JPEG files that are processed by the camera. If your digital photography workflow includes RAW images, you will need to use a RAW image-processing application such as Adobe Photoshop that supports color management.

NOTE ▶ The RAW digital image workflow is discussed in more detail in Lesson 5.

ColorSync in Professional Design Applications

Professional imaging and publishing applications, such as Adobe Photoshop, generally use their own color-management architecture. They may use some of ColorSync's features, but they include their own color-management features, functions, and preferences.

One easy way to determine whether an application implements its own color management is to see whether it includes color-management preferences. If it does, it's likely that the application or device is using its own system.

ColorSync provides value even with advanced or professional applications and devices. It is designed to check whether a document or image is being color managed; if not, it will manage the color, and if so, it will not touch the data.

Workflows that involve professional design and imaging applications and devices have many variables, and therefore it is more complicated to manage color in them. Lessons 5 through 8 of this book are focused on implementing color-managed workflows using popular applications and devices, including step-by-step exercises on how to set up applications and manage color through the process.

What You've Learned

- ColorSync works at the system level to automate color management in the applications and devices that support it.

- The ColorSync Utility is a centralized application for setting preferences, viewing installed profiles, assigning profiles to devices, and repairing profiles that do not conform to the ICC specification.

- Professional applications such as QuarkXPress and Adobe InDesign usually have their own capabilities and override or prevail over system-level color management, and you will have to learn how to use them.

- Professional design and imaging applications that do not support ColorSync instead use their own color management systems, which introduce complexity into the workflow.

3

Lesson Files Color Management in Mac OS X Book Files > Lessons > Lesson03

Time This lesson takes approximately 90 minutes to complete.

Goals Obtain and install generic profiles for your devices

Determine your printer's native color space

Choose a profile-creation service

Compare profiles from different sources

Print a target file for a company that will create profiles for your printer

Lesson **3**

Color Profile Basics

Profiles represent the color capabilities of your color-imaging devices. They are used by color management systems and applications to ensure predictable and accurate color reproduction. Therefore, the quality and accuracy of your profiles are crucial. Lesson 1 described what profiles are and what they are made of. In this lesson, we will explore the differences between generic and custom device profiles and look at the options for acquiring both types.

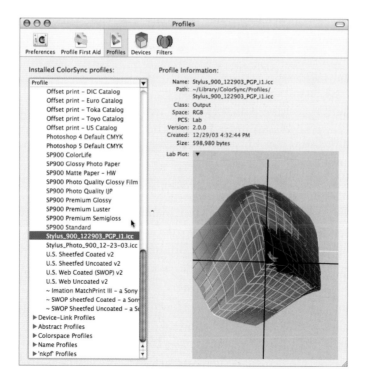

How Profiles Are Created

The process of making device profiles varies from device to device, and with the software you use, but the basic concept—that of *device characterization*—is the same regardless of the device.

With device characterization, color values from the device are measured with a dedicated instrument such as a colorimeter. Specialized software compares the measured values to the device-independent values of those colors, and stores this in a profile. The idea is to measure a wide range of colors—far more than you may think the device can reproduce—so that the software can determine the gamut of the device.

Creating profiles can range from being quick and painless to being involved and complex. It depends on the type of device being profiled, the tools being used to create the profiles, and your own knowledge level—it helps to understand some color-science terminology. In Lesson 4, we will walk through the characterization process for several types of devices to create custom profiles. But for now, let's focus on understanding and obtaining generic, or canned, profiles, as well as custom profiles created by a third party.

Understanding Generic Profiles

Today, most color devices come with device profiles created by the manufacturer. These are known as *generic,* or *canned,* profiles because they represent averaged data from a particular device model as it behaved in the factory. The manufacturer will typically follow the process described in the preceding section and in other lessons in this book to create profiles for its devices.

While generic profiles are convenient, the challenge is that, well, they're generic. Each physical unit of any given make and model of device is going to be slightly different from the others, and environmental factors and age will affect the device's color-reproduction capabilities as well. Generic profiles do not factor in such unique characteristics. In some cases, generic profiles aren't bad, particularly those for some desktop printers that are linear in response (well behaved) or have built-in calibration utilities. Indeed, some printer manufacturers include different profiles for the various types of ink and paper they manufacture. Using these profiles will definitely improve the predictability and accuracy of color reproduction. But for other devices, such as displays, generic profiles are going to have a minimal impact on your results.

Obtaining Generic Profiles

The first way to acquire generic profiles, as just explained, is from device manufacturers. Scanners, displays, and printers typically come with generic profiles that are installed automatically with the device software. In some cases, however, you may need to download the profiles separately. Some vendors make profiles available for download from their Web sites, including profiles for different printer paper and ink combinations.

There are other ways to obtain generic profiles. First, from imaging-software application developers. Most imaging applications include a set of profiles for common working spaces and devices. A good place to start is with Adobe Photoshop, which is likely to be the most common color-management application you will use.

Adobe Photoshop ships with a variety of profiles, including

- Adobe RGB (1998)
- Apple RGB
- ColorMatch RGB
- U.S. Web Coated (SWOP) v2
- U.S. Web Uncoated v2

- U.S. Sheetfed Coated v2
- U.S. Sheetfed Uncoated v2
- Euroscale Coated v2
- Euroscale Uncoated v2
- Japan Standard v2

NOTE ▶ If you're not using Adobe Photoshop (or any of Adobe's other professional design applications), Adobe has made many of these ICC profiles available on its Web site for download at www.adobe.com/support/downloads/main.html#ICC.

Another way to obtain generic profiles is through profiling services, service bureaus, and printers who have profiled their devices and presses and have made those profiles available on their Web sites. Other services offer a repository of profiles for different offset and digital photo printers. Dry Creek Photo, for example, offers a database of profiles at www.drycreekphoto.com for digital photo printers around the country—a useful resource if you outsource image printing.

Finally, there's, you guessed it, the Internet. A variety of Internet sites offer profiles, typically a combination of free and for-sale profiles. For example, the Seattle firm Chromix has an area on its Web site (www.chromix.com) where you can find and download profiles for a variety of devices, including printing presses.

Installing Generic Profiles

If you decide to use generic profiles to get your color-managed workflow rolling, choose one of the methods described in the preceding section to obtain one or more profiles for devices in your workflow and then perform the following steps to install them:

1   Download the profile or profiles from the Internet to your Desktop, or if the profiles come as part of an installer, double-click the Installer or Disk Image icon, and the profiles will be installed automatically.

2   If the profiles are not part of an installer, simply copy or drag them to the Macintosh HD > Library > ColorSync > Profiles directory, as shown in the following image. Installing in this location requires administrator privileges, and the profiles will be available to all users.

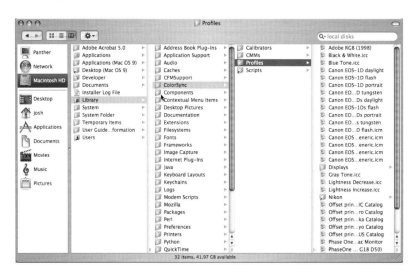

TIP If you do not want your profiles to be available to other users of your system, copy them to Macintosh HD > Users > *username* > Library > ColorSync > Profiles.

After you complete the installation, use the Color Sync Utility to verify that it installed correctly.

3 Navigate to Applications > Utilities and double-click the ColorSync Utility to launch it.

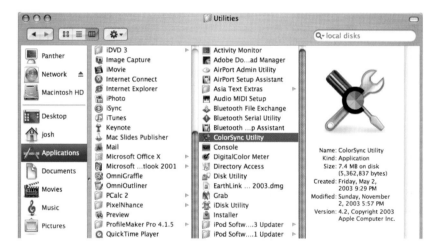

4 Click the Profiles icon.

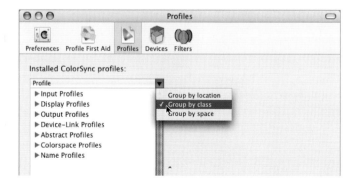

The Profiles section of the ColorSync Utility displays profiles grouped by location, class, or space. For this exercise, click the downward-pointing arrow and choose "Group by class." The ColorSync Utility groups installed profiles by the following classes: Input Profiles, Display Profiles, Output Profiles, Device-Link Profiles, Abstract Profiles, Colorspace Profiles, and Name Profiles.

5   Click the triangle next to the type of profile you just installed, such as Output Profiles.

6   Scroll down the list until you find the recently installed profile, and then click on its name to view information about the profile. A navigable 3D color model of the device's gamut is displayed on the right.

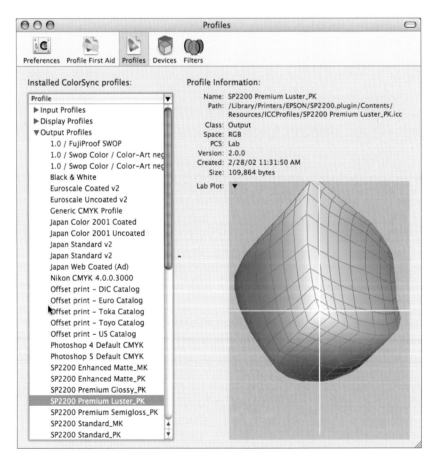

Understanding Custom Profiles

If you're serious about viewing and printing more accurate and predictable color, you will need to create *custom* profiles for your devices. Good custom profiles will capture the unique characteristics of your devices and therefore provide much better results.

So, how do you get good custom profiles? You can create them yourself, which you'll learn to do in Lesson 4, or you can pay someone else to make them for you. Let's explore that option now.

Selecting a Profile-Creation Service

If you want custom profiles without having to build them yourself, you can choose from two types of services: full-service providers and Internet-based mail-order services.

Like consultants, full-service providers come to your office or studio and create profiles for each of your devices and help set up your system. These services are typically expensive, but if you don't have the time or equipment to implement color management yourself, they present a viable option. Check with your service bureau for a list of providers.

Another option is to use a mail-order profiling service to create custom printer profiles. These services provide you with the target file for your printer type, along with printing instructions. You simply print the target and mail it off to the company. The chart is then measured with a spectrophotometer to obtain values for each color patch. Software is then used to compare measured data to the device-independent data. A short time later, you'll receive the profile (via e-mail or a Web site). If you use different paper and ink combinations, you can have profiles made for each combination. These services yield excellent results for a minimal investment—generally you can get a high-quality profile built for under $100.

Some profiling services will also create scanner and digital camera profiles, although this procedure is less straightforward. For example, you would have to send your digital camera to the company, which you may not want or be able to do. (Shipping aside, camera profiling has its own intrinsic challenges, which will be discussed in more detail in Lesson 4.) Scanners can be profiled more easily; the service sends you the target, and you send a scan of the target along with the target back to them. They generate the profile and provide it to you via e-mail or the Web.

Most profiling service providers will also create press profiles. The process is the same as desktop-printer profiling, except that the profiles are created using multiple targets, ideally from the beginning, middle, and end of the press run. The results are averaged into a single profile to accommodate variability throughout the press run. The profiles can also be created with different levels of black generation.

There are two potential challenges to be aware of with profiling services. First, it can be difficult to select a service and know that you're getting a good product. As with any other service, you should get references or a guarantee to ensure a high-quality product. Here are some questions to ask to help ascertain whether or not the service provider is dependable:

1   What type of device do you use to create profiles?

    The provider should be using a spectrophotometer. It doesn't need to be the most expensive, top-of-the-line model, but you want it to be a high-quality instrument.

2   How often do you calibrate this device?

    The device should be calibrated each time a target is measured.

3   Do you create multiple sets of measurements and average them out to reduce errors and anomalies?

    A profile created by measuring multiple targets and averaging the results is ideal but not essential. This is a feature of higher-end, more expensive services.

4   What type of validation do you perform on the profile?

    Ideally the profile is validated both by visual inspection and with software tools. Visual inspection involves printing a test image that includes a wide range of colors and examining it to ensure that there are no artifacts and that the image reproduces as expected. Software inspection tools will display the results in both curve and 3D charts, allowing comparisons with other profiles.

5   What type of guarantee do you offer?

You should get a money-back guarantee—but it's also your responsibility to make sure you know how to use the profile correctly.

Another issue to consider when purchasing output profiles from a specialized provider is that your printer's output may change over time, as the device itself ages or the manufacturer changes the inks or paper you use. This is called *drift*, because the color begins to drift from its original quality.

The likelihood and degree of drift really depend on the device and on the controls that the manufacturer uses in making the inks and paper. You can easily determine if there has been any drift in your printer by creating a reference file and reprinting it over time. For example, each time you change inks, you can print the reference file using the same settings and compare it to the original reference print. If the prints are different, your best option is have a new profile created.

> **NOTE** ▶ A reference file should contain a range of colors. A target used for creating profiles, such as the one used later in this lesson, can be a good reference. You can also create a reference file from your own images. For instructions on printing the reference file, follow the Printing Color-Managed Images exercise in Lesson 6.

Some service providers offer a subscription service to address this issue; you can pay an annual fee and have new profiles created several times a year.

Determining Your Printer's Native Color Space

Once you've selected a profile-creation service, obtain printing instructions and the appropriate profiling target for your printer, which can typically be found on the service's Web site. Most services will provide targets for both RGB and CMYK printers; you'll need to be sure to select the correct target for your device.

Desktop printers are either RGB or CMYK; printing presses are CMYK. The color mode of your printer is determined by the printer's driver or controller—not necessarily by the number of inks used to print. For example, most inkjet photo printers use six or seven inks but are considered RGB because the driver expects RGB data. If it receives anything else, it first converts it to RGB before converting to the printer's native space—a proprietary process handled in the driver. Printers that include a *RIP*, or raster image processor, such as PostScript, are typically CMYK.

If you're unsure whether your printer is RGB or CMYK, use the following exercise to check. To be safe, you can always send the service both the RGB and CMYK targets; it will be easy for them to determine the printer's correct color mode.

1   Launch Adobe Photoshop by clicking its application name or icon in the Applications folder of your hard drive or by clicking it in the Dock.

2   Choose File > Open, navigate to Color Management in Mac OS X Book Files > Lessons > Lesson03, and open the **CMYK vs RGB test.tif** file.

We will use this test file, provided by the profile-creation service provider Chromix, to determine if your printer is an RGB or CMYK device.

3   If Photoshop presents the Missing Profile dialog, select "Leave as is (don't color manage)."

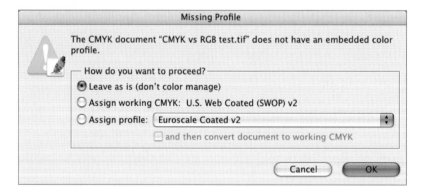

This tells Photoshop not to convert the file to a working space. We don't want to apply any color changes to the reference file.

4   Click OK.

Photoshop displays the reference file, an untagged CMYK file of a gray ramp.

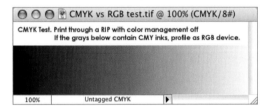

5   Choose File > Print with Preview.

6   In the Print dialog, check the Show More Options box, and choose Color Management from the pop-up menu just below it.

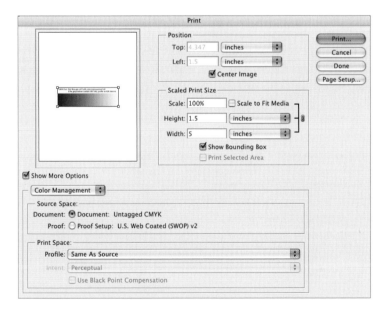

7   Under Source Space, make sure Document: Untagged CMYK is selected.

8   Under Print Space, choose Same As Source from the Profile pop-up menu. This ensures that Photoshop will send the file to the printer without any color management.

9 Click the Print button. The Print driver dialog appears.

10 Choose your color printer from the Printer pop-up menu, and then scroll through the Copies & Pages pop-up menu to locate your printer's media settings. The location of the media option varies with each printer; look for it under a heading such as Print Settings.

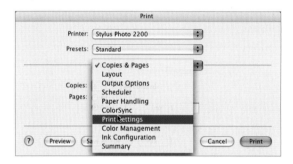

11 Select the correct paper for your device. The following image shows the Epson Print Settings menu, with Premium Glossy Photo Paper chosen from the Media Type pop-up menu. If you have the option, disable any automatic settings (such as by selecting Advanced Settings, as shown in the following figure).

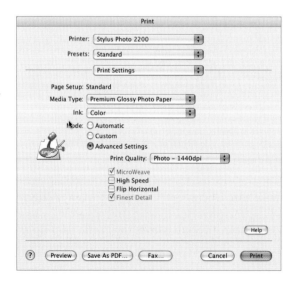

NOTE ► You may notice the ColorSync heading in the Copies & Pages pop-up menu. In this area you can specify a color conversion option and apply a Quartz filter. For all of the exercises in this book, we will leave these options set to their defaults: standard color conversion and no Quartz filter.

12 From the Copies & Pages pop-up menu locate your printer's color-management options, and *turn them off.* The location of these options varies with each printer; look for them under a heading such as Custom, Advanced, or Color Management. The following image shows the Color Management option in the Epson Stylus Photo 2200 printer driver, with No Color Adjustment selected.

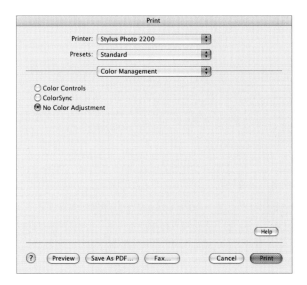

13 Click Print to start printing.

14 Inspect the printout. The file consists of a CMYK document with a gray (black) channel. If the printer is a true CMYK device, the gray ramp will print with black ink only and will appear neutral. If the gray ramp contains colored inks, then your printer is an RGB device and you should use the RGB target provided by the profiling service.

Printing a Target for Profiling

Although you may ultimately use a different service provider—or opt to create custom profiles, as you'll learn to do in Lesson 4—the following exercise walks you through Chromix's process of printing a target for a printer profile. You can complete this exercise using the RGB or CMYK target file included on this book's CD, depending on the native color space of your output device, and use the coupon on the CD to get a discount on your first set of profiles.

Even if you decide to acquire your printer profiles in a different way, you can follow along with this exercise to learn the typical process you would encounter with a profiling service.

1   Launch Adobe Photoshop by clicking its application name or icon in the Applications folder of your hard drive, or by clicking it in the Dock.

2   Choose File > Open and navigate to Color Management in Mac OS X Book Files > Lessons > Lesson03 folder on the CD.

3   Choose the appropriate target—either **CX CMYKx1 Profile Target.tif** for CMYK printers or **CX RGBx1 Profile Target.tif** for RGB printers—for your output device and click Open.

> **TIP** If you're unsure which target to use, complete the preceding exercise.

For my Epson Stylus 2200, I chose **CX RGBx1 Profile Target.tif**.

4   If Photoshop presents the Missing Profile dialog, select "Leave as is (don't color manage)." This tells Photoshop not to convert the file to a working space. Then click OK.

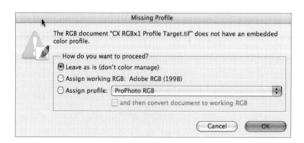

5 Ensure the file has opened correctly by checking the information area in the lower left of the image window. It should read Untagged RGB if you've opened the RGB target, or Untagged CMYK if you've opened the CMYK target.

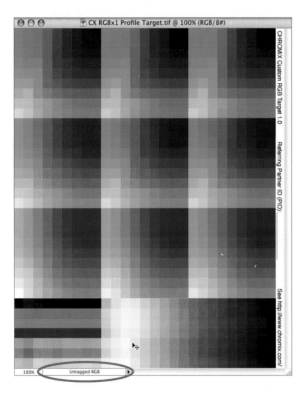

6 If the information area reads differently, choose Document Profile from the pop-up menu.

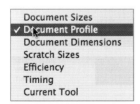

7 If the pop-up menu says Document Profile but the information area still doesn't say Untagged RGB/CMYK, choose Image > Mode > Assign Profile.

8 In the Assign Profile dialog, select Don't Color Manage This Document and click OK.

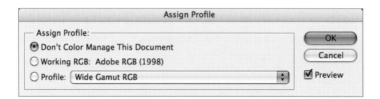

9 Check the information area again, choosing Document Profile from the pop-up menu if necessary. It should read Untagged RGB or Untagged CMYK.

Now we can print the target.

10 Choose File > Print with Preview.

11 In the Print dialog, check the Show More Options box and select Color Management from the pop-up menu just below it.

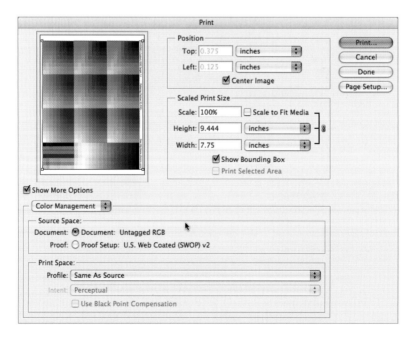

12 Under Source Space, choose Document: Untagged RGB (or Untagged CMYK), and under Print Space, choose Same As Source from the Profile pop-up menu. As with the preceding exercise, we're telling Photoshop not to color manage the file but rather to send it straight to the printer. The goal is to capture the printer's native gamut. If any color management is applied, the results will be affected.

13 Click Print, and in the Print driver dialog that appears, choose your printer from the list.

14 Choose your color printer from the Printer pop-up menu, and then scroll through the Copies & Pages pop-up menu to locate your printer's media settings. The location of the media option varies with each printer; look for it under a heading such as Print Settings.

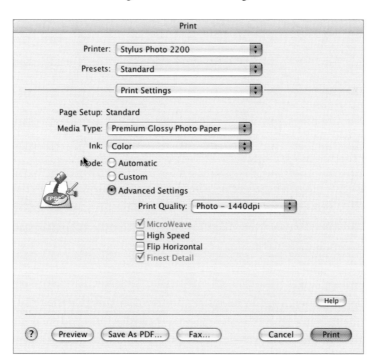

15 Select the correct paper for your device. The preceding image shows the Epson Print Settings menu, with Premium Glossy Photo Paper chosen from the Media Type pop-up menu. If you have the option, disable any automatic settings (such as by selecting Advanced Settings, also shown in the preceding figure).

16 From the Copies & Pages pop-up menu locate your printer's color-management options, and *turn them off.* The location of these options varies with each printer; look for them under a heading such as Custom, Advanced, or Color Management. The following image shows the Color Management option in the Epson Stylus Photo 2200 printer driver, with No Color Adjustment selected.

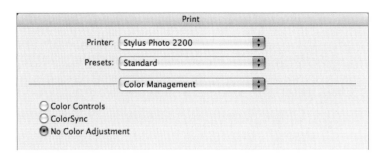

17 Click Print to start printing.

TIP Save these printer settings to use again when printing with the profile. It's important to always print with the same settings—changing the resolution or paper type will affect the results. To save them, choose Save As from the Presets menu.

18 Wait until the target is dry (30–45 minutes for inkjet prints) before putting it into an envelope, and be sure to protect it by covering the print side with a plain, blank sheet of paper. Enclose the order form and send it to Chromix. Don't forget to include the coupon from the CD in the envelope.

19 When you receive the profile back, install it on your hard drive as described in the Installing Generic Profiles exercise earlier in this lesson.

Comparing Profiles

Earlier in this lesson, you used the Mac OS X ColorSync Utility to check to make sure your color profiles were installed correctly. But you can also use it to compare different profiles. In this exercise, you'll compare a generic profile and a profile from the profile-creation exercise to see how they differ.

1   Double-click on the ColorSync Utility, located in the Applications > Utilities folder of your hard drive, to launch it.

2   Click the Profiles icon and select the profile for your printer from the list of installed ColorSync profiles. You can select a generic profile for your printer that came with the printer, or one downloaded from the Internet.

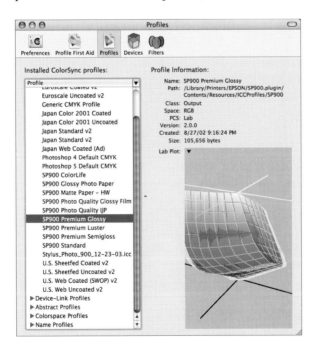

Details about the profile and a 3D rendering of its color gamut are displayed on the right of the window.

3   Click the triangle in the Lab Plot area and choose "Hold for comparison" from the pop-up menu.

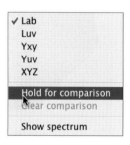

4   Now choose a different printer profile: a profile created for you by Chromix, one of the sample profiles included on this book's CD, or one of the standards, such as U.S. Sheetfed Coated v2.

> **NOTE** ▶ You will first have to install one or more of these sample profiles on your hard drive before they appear on this list.

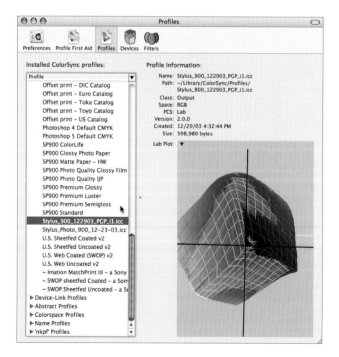

The ColorSync Utility overlays two profiles in the 3D preview area, as shown in the preceding figure, comparing the two printer profiles you selected. Your preview may look different from mine, depending on which profiles you selected to compare. I chose the generic SP Premium Glossy profile that came with my Epson Stylus Photo 2200 and an Epson profile I created called Stylus_900_122903_PGP_i1.icc.

The areas on the outside of the cube, in white, and the dark section cross-cutting the cube are areas where the Chromix profile has more data than the generic Epson profile—data that contains more color.

What You've Learned

- Profiles are created by comparing measured values from a device with device-independent color values.

- Generic profiles don't factor in the unique characteristics of your specific device and are thus of limited usefulness.

- There are three different ways to get profiles for your device: use generic profiles from the manufacturer, pay to have profiles created, or create them yourself.

- Printer profiling services provide a cost-effective way to obtain custom profiles for your imaging devices, such as printers.

4

Lesson Files	Color Management in Mac OS X Book Files > Lessons > Lesson04
Time	This lesson takes approximately 2 hours to complete.
Goals	Identify the three major color-measurement devices
	Create custom profiles for your display using three techniques
	Create custom digital camera, scanner, and printer profiles using external calibrators and software
	Compare generic and custom color profiles

Creating Custom Profiles

To get the best results and most predictability from color management, you need to create your own device profiles. While this may seem like a daunting process, it can be relatively easy to do, and the results are well worth the effort. There is a wide range of profiling products on the market; some of these are reasonably priced, easy to use, and able to profile most types of devices.

Profiling products range from standalone products made specifically for a certain type of device, to profiling "suites," such as the GretagMacbeth Eye-One bundle and the X-RiteColor Ensemble, which include a measurement device and software that can profile scanners, cameras, displays, printers, and even projectors.

The choice of profiling package depends on your own criteria: how much it costs, how easy it is to use, what advanced features it includes, and the quality of its results. Some professionals believe that packages that take the Swiss Army knife all-in-one approach don't do as good a job at creating profiles as programs that are dedicated to creating a specific type of profile. In any case, this lesson uses a variety of applications to create device profiles. These are not the only or necessarily the best products available; rather, they represent an assortment of solutions.

Understanding Measurement Devices

To calibrate displays and printers, a measurement device is required. There are a variety of devices on the market, each with different capabilities. Buying a measurement device is a complicated process in itself, and should you prefer to skip the color babble, a decent spectrophotometer such as the GretagMacbeth Eye-One will handle all of your color-management needs. Three basic types of devices are used in graphic arts and publishing, as described below.

- *Densitometer*—A densitometer measures the density of ink on paper (that is, the absorption of light), not color values. A densitometer can tell you how much of a color is on the page, but not what the color is. This is useful for a variety of purposes: to check whether the printing devices are behaving, for example, or to calibrate a device. Densitometers can be found on or near every printing press, but they are not useful for creating device profiles.

- *Colorimeter*—A colorimeter measures the color value of a sample, using color filters, within a specific color space. A colorimeter can determine if two colors are the same; it does not, however, take into account the light under which the samples are measured. Colorimeters are often used to calibrate both LCD and CRT display types.

- *Spectrophotometer*—A spectrophotometer measures the wavelength of light across the entire visible spectrum of colors. This type of measurement is the broadest, and it can easily be translated into a number of values, including those used by colorimeters and densitometers. As it can be used to profile both displays and printers, the spectrophotometer is preferred for device profiling.

These devices typically come in different flavors; some measure one patch of color at a time, while others measure strips in an automated fashion. The automated devices cost more—sometimes much more—but save time and reduce errors. Some devices, such as the GretagMacbeth Eye-One spectrophotometer, can measure single patches but also include an attachment that enables the device to engage a strip-reading mode. Spend some time creating profiles with a device that only measures patch by patch, and you will quickly come to appreciate the value of an automated instrument. In case you were wondering, the Rolls-Royce of these devices is the GretagMacbeth iCColor spectrophotometer—simply feed a target into the device, wait about 20 seconds, and the measurements are complete, all for about $5,000.

> **NOTE ▶** You can use the trial applications on this book's CD to complete the exercises in this lesson even if you don't have a color-measurement device.

Creating Display Profiles

The display is where color professionals spend most of their time viewing color information, and where they evaluate and adjust color data. And it just so happens to be the easiest device to profile. Creating a custom profile for your display will have a dramatic effect and will enable you to use your display as a predictor of your output-device results.

Choosing High-Quality Displays

When investing in a display for high-quality color-managed workflows, one of the primary considerations is whether to choose LCD or CRT technology. Color professionals disagree as to which is better for color reproduction. Flat panels, which are now the only type of display that Apple sells, tend to have more contrast than CRTs, and the viewing angle may affect the appearance of the color data.

Regardless of whether you choose CRT or flat-panel technology, keep in mind that as with most things in life, you get what you pay for. So caveat emptor: "bargain" displays simply don't have the quality or response required for accurate color reproduction.

Ultimately, it's a matter of personal preference. Just be sure that for color management, you use a high-quality display. "High" quality is subjective, but generally it includes a small dot pitch (the distance between the dots onscreen), support for high-resolution modes, and controls for color temperature and geometry.

Displays degrade with age, becoming less bright and less reliable for viewing color data over time. If your display is more than three years old, and you're dissatisfied with its handling of color data, consider a new display.

> **NOTE ▶** If you use an LCD (flat panel) monitor, ensure that any measurement device you use is designed for an LCD or includes an LCD adapter. Devices with suction cups can damage LCDs.

Characterization vs. Calibration

When implementing color management, you often encounter the terms *calibration* and *characterization,* which can be confusing, but the difference is really quite simple: *calibration* changes a device to a standard or to a known state, while *characterization* is the process of measuring the characteristics of the device and creating a profile. Most display color-management products do both tasks, so the terms are often used interchangeably. If your profiling product doesn't do both simultaneously, or if you're using different tools for each, just remember to calibrate first, then characterize.

You can calibrate and characterize a display in three ways, which increase in price and quality: using visual calibration, using a display calibrator, and using a calibrated display system. After discussing how each method works, we will create and compare profiles using visual profiling and an external display calibrator.

Visual Calibration

In visual calibration, your eyes are the measurement tool. Although visual calibration does an excellent job of factoring in ambient lighting conditions in the profiling process, this method is very subjective and is more prone to errors and inconsistencies than device-based calibration. If your goal is to create consistency among multiple displays—say, across all the displays in a production shop—or consistency across time, then visual calibration may not be the best solution, as you have no objective reference point.

Apple ships a very effective (and free) visual characterization tool with Mac OS X: the Display Calibrator Assistant. We will use it shortly to both calibrate and characterize your display.

Display Calibrators

Display calibrators use a measurement device along with software to profile your display. This approach is automated and much less subjective than visual calibration, in which you adjust the controls until the onscreen image appears a certain way. The software flashes a range of colors on the screen, which are measured by the device. The results are compared with the known values of the various colors, and a profile is created that accounts for the particular results of your display. In most cases, a profile created with a display calibrator will be more accurate (and more expensive) than one created using visual calibration.

Calibrated Display Systems

The ultimate solution for a color-accurate display (which also happens to be the most expensive) is a *calibrated display system*. Calibrated display systems typically include a very high-quality monitor, a measurement device, software, and a hood to shield the display from ambient light (a good idea regardless of which type of system you use), all designed to work together. What makes these systems so accurate is the integration of display, software, and calibrator. The software communicates with the display and your graphics card and makes adjustments in the display *automatically*. Calibrated display systems such as the Sony Artisan and the Barco Reference Calibrator V are easy to use and provide better results than visual calibration or third-party display calibrators. With a calibrated display system, there is no guesswork involved, no loss of brightness and gamut. If color is a critical component of your work, and you can afford one of these systems, buy one.

The Sony Artisan is an example of a calibrated display system.

The Sony Artisan software, for example, clearly indicates the calibration status of the display, including the target color space, calibration results (including the date of the last calibration), and display configuration details. If the display is out of calibration, a warning alerts the user at startup as well in the Artisan application.

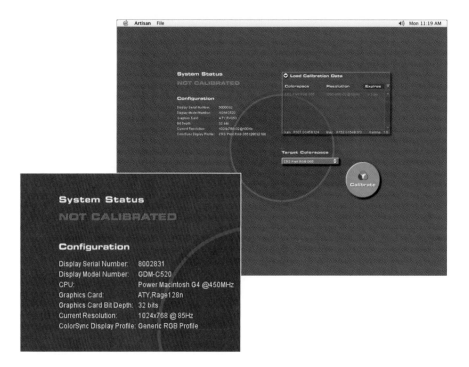

Preparing to Profile Your Display

We're almost ready to create and compare some display profiles. But first, take a moment to do a few things to increase the accuracy of the profile.

- Let your display warm up. For CRTs, that's a minimum of 30 minutes, preferably one hour. For LCDs, 5 to 10 minutes should suffice.

- Turn off screen savers and energy-saving settings. These can interrupt the process.

- Determine your display's settings: resolution, refresh rate, geometry, and bit depth, and *don't change the settings* (either through the display's front-panel controls or through the operating system). If you change the settings, you should re-profile the display.

- Set the Desktop to a neutral gray.

- Set the white point to 5000k (D50) or 6500k (D65), if supported by your display. The overall goal is to match the tonal reproduction characteristics of your display to the intended viewing conditions and output.

  NOTE ▶ LCDs and laptop displays typically lack controls for white point.

- Clean your display using a product specifically formulated for displays. Most office supply stores carry this type of product.

- Avoid bright light directed at the display. Use a display hood, if available.

Using Visual Calibration to Create a Display Profile

Let's create a profile for your display using Apple's Display Calibrator Assistant, a visual-profiling tool.

1   Open System Preferences by clicking its icon in the Dock, and then click the Displays icon.

2   Click the Color tab.

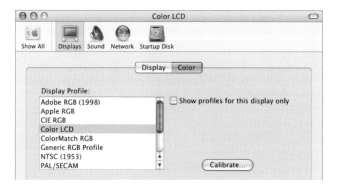

3   Click the Calibrate button, and the Introduction screen appears.

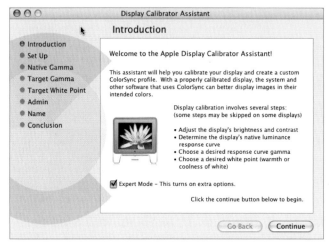

The Introduction screen provides an overview of the Display Calibrator Assistant and the steps required to use it.

4   Make sure the Expert Mode box is checked. Although the Expert Mode is more involved, it gives you more options and produces better results.

5   Click Continue. The Native Gamma window appears.

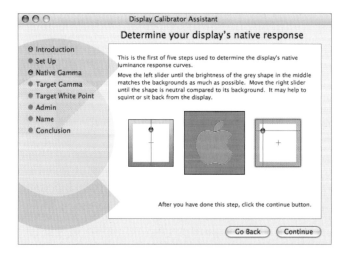

This is the first window for a five-step adjustment in the assistant, designed to determine the *luminance* of your display. Luminance is the amount of light emitted by the display.

The assistant uses two sliders to determine luminance. Each slider control has a border that indicates the change made by moving the slider a certain direction. For example, on the brightness box (on the left), moving the slider up increases the brightness; moving it down decreases the brightness. The border of the control is lighter at the top, darker at the bottom. The control on the right, which affects color balance, shows the change in color made by moving the slider toward the direction of a color on the border.

6   Adjust the left slider until the brightness of the Apple icon matches the surrounding boxed background. Move the slider all the way up and all the way down, and then narrow in on the spot that you think achieves the best match. Next, move the right slider until the color of the Apple icon appears most neutral. Again, move the slider around liberally and then home in on the spot that appears to have the least amount of color in the Apple icon.

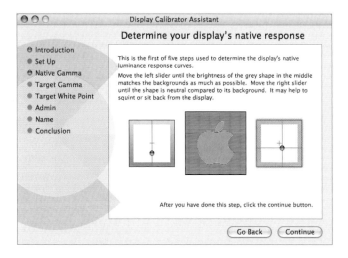

TIP ▶ Keep in mind that this is a very subjective process, and there is no right or wrong answer—simply make the best choice you can. As the instructions note, it does help to sit back and squint your eyes a bit.

7 When you are satisfied with the adjustments, click Continue.

8 Repeat steps 6 and 7 four more times as prompted by the assistant, each time further homing in on the luminance of your display as part of the native gamma adjustments.

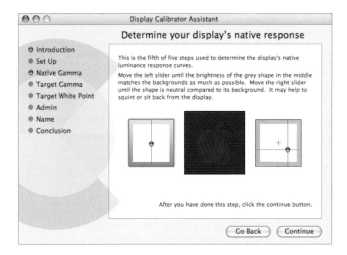

9 When the Apple icon essentially blends in with its background, click Continue to move to the target gamma adjustment.

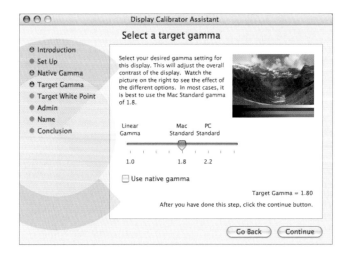

Gamma is the ratio of contrast that is displayed. The higher the number, the more contrast you will see.

10 Adjust the slider back and forth, watching the changes that occur in the test image, until you see a good balance between highlights and shadows. Use the clouds to examine the changes in the highlights, and the darker parts of the mountains to examine the shadow detail.

At the ideal setting, the tonal gradations in the color bars should be smooth, all the way from bright highlights to deep shadows.

The numbers underneath the slider represent the contrast ratio. Notice that there is a difference between Macintosh and Windows gamma settings. If you are using the Display Calibrator Assistant with the intention of matching displays between the two platforms, consider selecting the same gamma on both systems. You will likely have a better match across the Mac and Windows platforms if you use the PC Standard gamma of 2.2.

> **TIP** If you are unsure about this setting, set the slider at Mac Standard.

11 When you finish, click Continue. The Target White Point adjustment window appears.

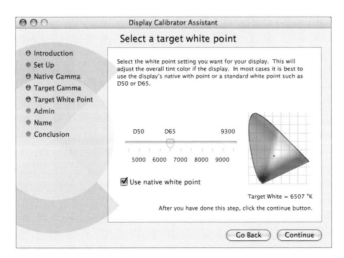

White point is the color temperature of the display, measured in kelvins. The higher the white point, the bluer the white will appear; the lower the white point, the redder the white will appear.

To understand this concept, notice the light at different times of the day. During the morning and evening, when the sun is low on the horizon, the light is warm and rich in color, or about 3500 kelvins. In the middle of the day, when the sun is overhead, the light is cooler, about 6500 kelvins. These temperatures are often noted as D50 (for 5000) or D65 (for 6500).

Most professional proofing systems and color-correct viewing booths used by printers and photographers use D50 lights to simulate daylight. D50 was established as the prepress industry standard, although new standards are emerging based on D65. The challenge with this, however, is that printed materials and photographs will be viewed under many light conditions. It's important to choose a setting that your display can actually reproduce. D50 may also make your display appear dim and yellow. As a result, many users select D65, which results in a much closer match to your output device.

12 Check the "Use native white point" box to use the white point that was determined by the selections you made in the first steps of the process.

NOTE ▶ Much like the target gamma setting, the white point differs between Macintosh and Windows systems. Macintosh users will see the best results by setting their displays to a D50 white point and a gamma of 1.8. PC users will see the best results by setting their displays to D65 and a gamma of 2.2. The exception to this rule is when both a Macintosh and a PC are used in the same color-managed workflow. In this scenario, the best results will be achieved by using a device calibrator or calibrated display system set to the same white point and gamma on both systems.

13 Click Continue. The Administrator window appears.

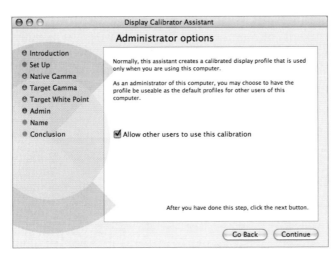

Administrator options, enabled by the Expert Mode box checked in step 4, let you share your profile with other users of the system.

14 Check the "Allow other users to use this calibration" box if you want others to be able to share this profile.

15 Click Continue.

16 In the window that appears, name the profile, giving it a meaningful name that will distinguish this profile from others for the same device. For example, include the device name and its calibration settings.

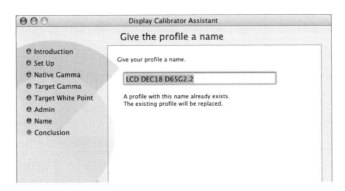

17 Click Continue.

Congratulations! You have just created a custom profile that factors in the unique characteristics of your display, determined by the measurement instrument—your eyes. The Conclusion screen that appears summarizes the relevant details of the profile, which can be useful in comparing these results to generic profiles for the device, an exercise that you'll perform later in this chapter.

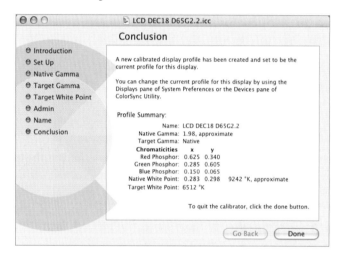

Note the difference between Native Gamma and Target Gamma in this window. The profile you just created compensates for the differences between the native and desired gammas.

18 Click Done to close the Display Calibrator Assistant.

The Color tab of the Displays System Preferences window appears, with the profile you just created selected from the Display Profile list. The display profile will be used by applications that support ColorSync to determine which display profile to use.

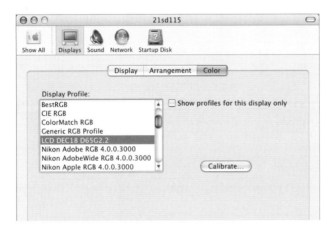

Using a Calibrator to Create a Display Profile

This exercise uses the GretagMacbeth Eye-One Match to demonstrate how to calibrate and characterize, or profile, a display with a display calibrator. If you don't have a calibrator, or have a different product, you can still follow this exercise to learn the general process.

1   Launch Eye-One Match by double-clicking its icon in the Applications folder of your hard drive. The home screen appears.

The home screen shows the types of devices that the software can profile: displays (also called *monitors*), projectors, scanners, and printers. The Eye-One tool is very easy to use: help is available from every screen, and the interface leaves little room for error.

2   Since we are creating a display profile, click the icon that looks like an Apple Cinema Display.

3   Select the Advanced Profiling Mode, which allows you to chose the white point and gamma of your display; we'll do that later in this exercise.

4   Click the right arrow in the lower right of the screen to begin.

The first step in profiling is to calibrate the measurement device.

5   Place the Eye-One device on its base, which includes a reference target, and click Calibrate to calibrate the device.

Eye-One compares the results with the known value of the calibration patch and makes any adjustments as needed.

NOTE ▶ Not all calibrators include this step, particularly devices that calibrate only displays.

6   Click the right arrow to choose your display calibration settings.

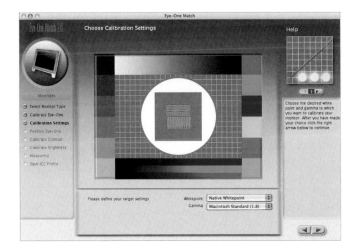

This is where you can choose the white point and gamma of your display.

NOTE ▶ If your display has the capability to set the white point via the hardware controls, set the display setting before calibrating.

7   Click and hold to view the Whitepoint pop-up menu.

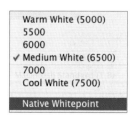

The Whitepoint selection determines the color of the white of the display. The device will measure the actual or native white point of the display, and then the software will adjust the display to achieve the desired white point (or a point as close to it as possible). The higher the number, the cooler (or bluer) the white; the lower the number, the warmer (or redder) the white. The Native Whitepoint setting instructs the software to use the measured white-point value. This is often a good choice for displays that lack the controls to select a white point, particularly LCDs. As noted previously, the typical setting for the Mac is 5000 (also called D50). However, the D50 setting is based on press output; desktop printer users will likely have better results with D65.

8   Experiment with the various settings to see how they change your computer display, and then choose Medium White (6500).

9   Click and hold on the Gamma pop-up menu.

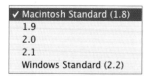

The Gamma selection determines the relationship between light and dark values, similar to contrast.

10 Leave the Gamma setting at Macintosh Standard (1.8).

11 Click the right arrow and place the measurement device on the display. As it calibrates and plots the gamut, the software will display and measure a wide range of color values.

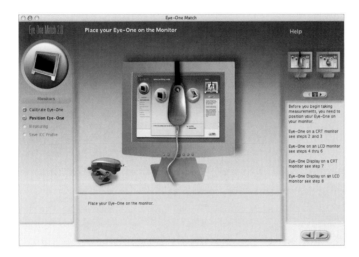

If you use an LCD such as the Apple Cinema Display or a PowerBook, make sure that your calibration device is safe to use on an LCD. The suction cups on devices designed for CRTs can damage the LCD. Most manufacturers have an adapter, or a version that specifically works on LCDs.

Also, if you're using an LCD, be sure to use the appropriate attachment, which usually hangs the device with a counterweight. If you are using a CRT, the attachment will typically have suction cups that will stick to the glass. Once the device is attached, the software first automatically detects where on the screen the sensor is located, and then begins the measurement (some products may require you to manually start the process).

12 When the process is complete, the Save ICC Profile window appears. Save the profile with a name that includes the calibration settings, and then click the right arrow button. In this example, the profile was named with the device name and date.

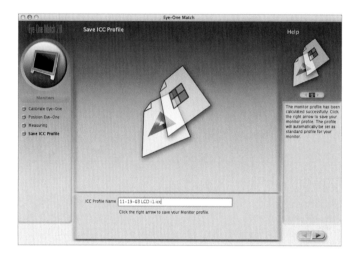

The software indicates that the profile has been saved and that the profile has now been set as the standard profile.

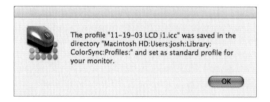

13 Click OK, and close the Eye-One Match application.

14 Open the Displays System Preferences panel, and click the Color tab.

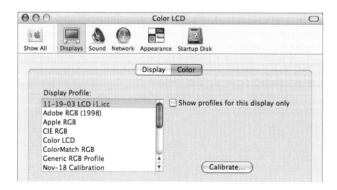

Your new profile is in the Display Profile list and is selected as the default display profile.

NOTE ▶ If your profiling product does not automatically set the display profile, you will need to change it by selecting the correct profile from the list.

Comparing Display Profiles

Now that you have at least two display profiles—the default profile included with your display and the profile created with the Apple Display Calibrator Assistant—we can compare them. If your display didn't come with a default profile, then use one of the profiles included with ColorSync; this is simply an exercise to illustrate the value of creating a custom profile.

1   Launch the ColorSync Utility inside the Applications > Utilities folder on your hard drive.

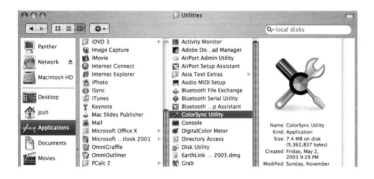

2   Click the Profiles icon.

On the left, the utility displays a list of all of the profiles installed on your system, organized by category.

NOTE ▶ If your list of installed ColorSync profiles appears different from what's shown in the preceding image, click the downward-pointing triangle on the Profile list box and choose "Group by class."

3   Click the triangle next to Display Profiles, and select a display profile, such as Color LCD.

Information about this profile appears on the right. Notice the location, color space, creation date, size, and other information about this profile, including its Lab Plot 3D visual representation.

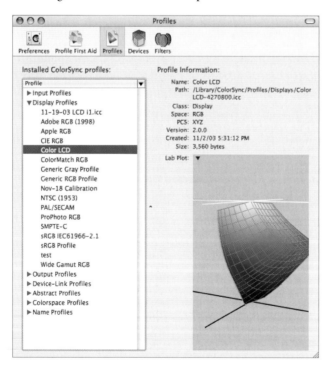

4   Click and drag on the 3D color model to view this profile's color space from multiple angles, then release the mouse.

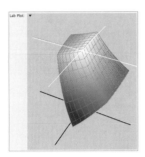 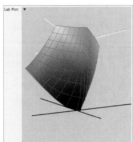

5   Click the triangle in the Lab Plot area and choose "Hold for comparison" from the pop-up menu.

6   Choose the profile you created with the Apple Display Calibrator Assistant (or one you created with your external display calibrator) from the left-hand list. The ColorSync Utility displays an overlay plot of the two profiles.

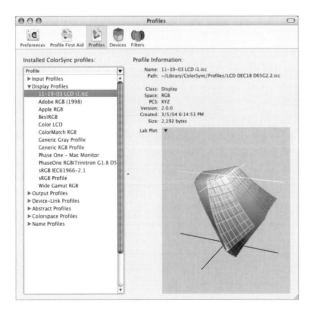

The ghosted white outline in the figure is the first, generic profile.

7   Click and drag the cursor over the color model to see how the profiles compare throughout the range of colors displayed by the 3D color model.

Notice whether the color gamut of my custom profile is larger than that of the default profile—meaning that it includes more colors. If the custom profile includes more data, it will be more accurate when used for soft-proofing. In some cases, the differences between two profiles may be very slight, and you will not be able to see any variation in the color model.

You can compare any two profiles with the ColorSync Utility, which is a useful way to visualize the differences between the color gamuts of two devices.

Ensuring Consistency Across Displays

If one of your goals is to have consistency across multiple displays in your workflow, for example in a studio, the simplest way to reduce variability is to use the same make and model of display and the same calibration system at each workstation. If you choose to go with an external display calibrator, you can save money by purchasing one physical device (or a few if you have a lot of systems) and running the software on each monitor. Just be sure to check the manufacturer's policy about software licensing—you may need a license for each computer.

Whichever approach you select to calibrate displays, be sure to use *only that method* to create a profile for each display. Consistency is one of the keys to successful color management.

Keeping Profiles Accurate

A good rule of thumb is to recalibrate your display once a week: calibration is easy, free, and effective. It's also a good idea to recalibrate prior to any important color work—say, a big job.

Creating Digital Camera Profiles

Creating a profile for a digital camera is easy; creating a good profile is another story. With input devices such as scanners, variability over time is low: the light source is fixed, and each scan uses the same source. The challenge with creating camera profiles is that there are a lot of variables—most of which change with each photograph.

Lighting poses the biggest challenge. In the studio, lights have qualities, such as color temperature and luminance, that change over time and with each photo shoot. Simply moving a studio light will change the lighting conditions. In the field, lighting changes by the minute as the sun moves across the sky. And like other devices, each camera has its own subtle characteristics.

As a result, many experts contend that it's only worth the effort to profile digital cameras if you are a studio photographer with highly controlled lighting setups. They believe it's easier, faster, and cheaper to bring digital photographs into a color-managed workflow using generic and working-space profiles.

Indeed, profiles cannot compensate for all variability and are not meant to eliminate the need for image editing. Even for digital cameras, however, profiles can reduce the amount of time needed to color edit an image by as much as 85 to 90 percent. If you choose to profile your camera, the trick is to determine which solution works best for you. Following are the three most common options for profiling cameras.

1 Use a working space instead of a camera profile.

The simplest option is to convert your images to a working-space profile when you edit it. If your display is calibrated and you are consistent with your workflow, you will be able to use soft-proofing (camera workflow and soft-proofing of images are covered in detail in Lessons 5 and 6) to predict what the image will look like in print.

Certain cameras, particularly digital single-lens reflex models, enable you to select the working-space profile for the camera. Once an image is taken, an in-camera process converts the image from the camera's native color space (usually a generic profile for that model of camera) to the selected working space and embeds that profile in the image. This option is typically limited to one or two working-space profiles, such as AdobeRGB or sRGB.

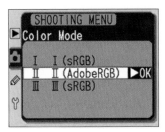

The Nikon D100 digital single-lens reflex camera has three Color Mode options: AdobeRGB, which converts the image to the same working space used in Photoshop, and two sRGB profiles.

In conjunction with the working-space profiles, it's a good idea to create a custom white balance for each scene being photographed. Additionally, working in RAW format enables greater flexibility during editing.

NOTE ▶ If you chose to create a custom profile for your camera, disable the use of a working space within the camera to avoid double color management (transforming the image twice), which will produce poor results.

2   Use the camera-profiling feature of your profiling software.

The process is simple: shoot an image of the target in each scene. Before you process the images, create a profile from each shot of the target, and use it as the source profile for the image. The results may vary; most photographers find that the results are flat and lack contrast, or that the profile simply doesn't do the job and doesn't warrant the time required.

3   Use a profiling package designed specifically for digital cameras, such as Integrated Color Corp.'s ColorEyes 20/20.

In the case of ColorEyes 20/20, you only have to create the profile once—regardless of the lighting conditions—for each camera. The trick is to light the target precisely as instructed. While this requires a bit of time and patience, many photographers have found it to be worth the effort—especially for studio photography. There are several key features in this package: a specialized target; an extremely specific process for lighting and photographing the target; use of the camera's gray balance in profile creation; and finally, a profile-generating algorithm specifically designed for digital cameras.

NOTE ▶ Lessons 5 and 6 go into greater detail about the use of camera profiles and working spaces in Adobe Photoshop.

Creating a Digital Camera Profile, Take One

This exercise uses GretagMacbeth's ProfileMaker 4.1 Professional to create a digital camera profile. If you have not already installed the trial version of ProfileMaker Professional from this book's CD, do so now before beginning the exercise.

1   Launch ProfileMaker Professional and select the digital camera module by clicking the Camera icon.

The first step is to select the reference file, which contains the expected measurement data for the target in use. The profiling software will compare the actual data from the photograph of the target to the reference data in order to build the profile.

2   Choose **ColorChecker DC.txt** as your reference target file from the Reference pop-up menu.

Next, you will select the target image—the actual target data from your camera.

3   Choose Open from the Sample pop-up menu.

4   In the Open dialog that appears, navigate to and select the file
ColorChecker-D100.tif in the Color Management in Mac OS X Book
Files > Lessons > Lesson04 folder on your hard drive. If you have access
to a ColorChecker DC or other target, use an actual image from your
camera rather than the included sample image.

When you select the image, it opens automatically in another window that allows you to adjust the crop.

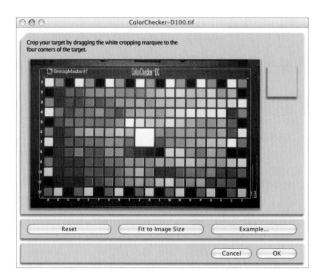

5   Crop the target by adjusting the marquee so that the selection includes only the color patch (exclude the grayscale patches that border the target). It's important to crop the image as described so that extraneous data, such as that from the grayscale patches, does not affect the profile creation. Click the Example button to see the exact crop. The Reset button will reset the marquee to the default settings, while the Fit to Image Size button will adjust the image of the target to fit into the crop window.

6   When you have adjusted all four corners, click OK to return to the Camera tab of the main interface.

7   Now you're ready to create the profile. Click Start.

   ProfileMaker Pro displays a Save dialog and prompts you for a profile name.

   NOTE ▶ The demonstration version of ProfileMaker Professional included on this book's CD will not save the profile. The full version of the application is required to save profiles.

8   Give the profile a meaningful name.

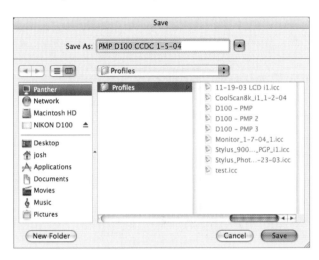

In this example, the profile name is "PMP D100 CCDC 1-5-04." *PMP* indicates that it was created using ProfileMaker Professional; *D100* indicates that the profile is for a Nikon D100 camera; *CCDC* stands for the ColorChecker DC target; and *1-5-04* is the date it was created.

NOTE ▶ ProfileMaker Professional automatically selects the ColorSync Profiles directory to save the profile. If you use a different camera-profile utility, be sure to store your profile in this directory.

9   Click Save. ProfileMaker Professional generates the profile. Depending on the speed of your Mac, it will take approximately one minute. When finished, ProfileMaker Professional returns to the Camera window. Quit the application when finished.

Creating a Digital Camera Profile, Take Two

The following exercise uses the ColorEyes 20/20 Adobe Photoshop plug-in and a sample target included on this book's CD to create a digital camera profile. If you have not already installed ColorEyes 20/20 from the CD, do so now.

1   Launch Adobe Photoshop and choose File > Open.

2   Navigate to the **Sample Camera Capture Target.tif** file in the Color Management in Mac OS X Book Files > Lessons > Lesson04 folder on your hard drive, and click Open.

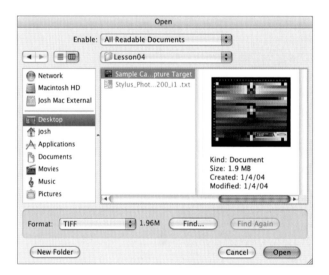

NOTE ▶ A photograph of the ColorEyes target is included on this book's CD for this exercise. If you have purchased ColorEyes, you can photo-graph the target yourself as described in the user manual and open that image of the target, instead of the sample file.

3 If Photoshop displays the Missing Profile alert, select "Leave as is (don't color manage)" and then click OK. This tells Photoshop not to convert the file to a working space, as we don't want to apply any color changes to the target.

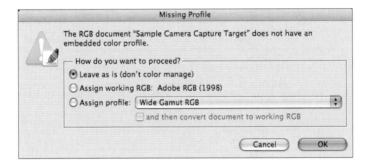

4 To ensure that the file has opened correctly, look at the lower-left corner of the image window. The name of the working space should be displayed: Untagged RGB. If it is, skip to step 9.

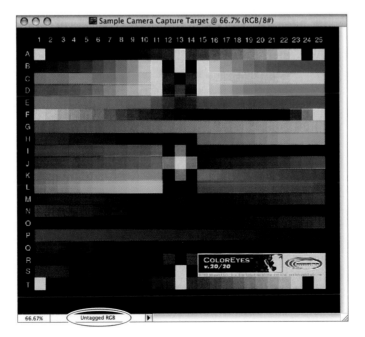

5   If the profile name does not display, or if Photoshop displays an incorrect profile, click the right-pointing arrow and select Document Profile from the pop-up menu.

6   If Untagged RGB now appears, skip to step 9. If not, choose Image > Mode > Assign Profile.

7   In the Assign Profile dialog, select the Don't Color Manage This Document option and then click OK.

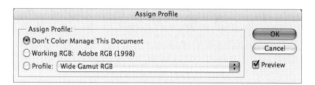

8   Once again, choose Document Profile from the image window's pop-up menu, and Untagged RGB should now display.

9   To launch the ColorEyes plug-in, select Filter > Integrated Color > ColorEyes.

10 To provide ColorEyes with the appropriate reference file for the target image, click the Choose Reference File button in ColorEyes' main window.

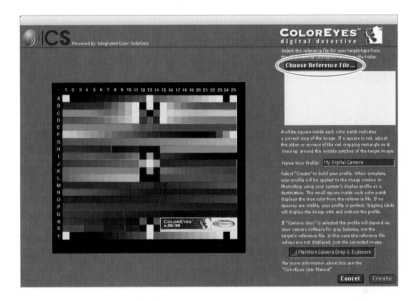

The Choose a File dialog appears, enabling you to choose a reference file.

11 Navigate to the target reference file **Sample Camera Target Reference File.cie,** located in Macintosh HD > Color Management in Mac OS X Book Files > Lessons > Lesson04.

This file contains the known values for the target, which will be compared to the values from the image of the target taken with a digital camera.

12 Click Choose. ColorEyes now displays a grid overlaid on the target image. The grid tells the software where each of the patches are on the target, so that the software can accurately process the data. It's important to properly position the grid.

13 Adjust the corners by dragging the square red handles of the grid until all of the gray corner squares have a green dot.

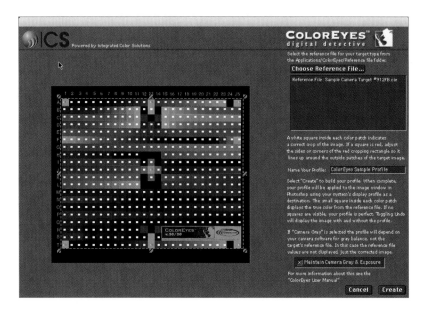

14 Next, check the Maintain Camera Gray & Exposure box in the lower-right area of the ColorEyes window.

This instructs ColorEyes to use the gray balance from the camera, resulting in a profile that will correct hue and saturation values but will leave gray and exposure values untouched.

15 Give your profile an intuitive name in the Name Your Profile box, and then click Create.

ColorEyes processes the data and creates the profile, which is automatically added to the ColorSync profile library, and returns you to Photoshop's main interface.

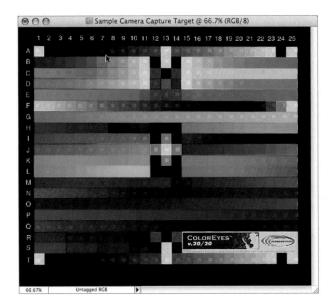

16 Close the image window or quit Photoshop without saving the file. The target has been modified to illustrate the changes that were made in creating the profile.

These exercises demonstrate two approaches to creating camera profiles; using camera profiles as part of a color-managed workflow will be covered in depth in Lesson 5. Remember, digital cameras are perhaps the most difficult devices to profile. The challenge is to photograph the target properly to create an accurate profile. The benefits of camera profiles will be realized only when a high-quality profile is both created and used in a color-managed workflow. If you are just getting started with color management, you may consider first profiling just your display and printer(s) to establish a color-managed workflow, and then later, if you encounter inconsistencies and unpredictable outcomes with digital images, profile your camera.

Creating Scanner Profiles

Scanner profiles improve the consistency and predictability of your color images and save you time. Creating scanner profiles is easy and straightforward: you scan a target, and the profiling software compares the scan to reference data for that target and generates a profile.

To create a profile for your scanner, you will need profiling software, a target, and the target reference file. Ideally, you want the target to be the same film or paper type as the original you're scanning. For example, if you're scanning a print (also known as a *reflective* image), your target should be reflective; if your image is on transparency or film (also known as a *transmissive* image), your target should be transmissive.

> **NOTE ▶** There are no targets for negative film. This is largely due to the challenge of scanning negatives, caused by the orange mask in the negative.

The most common target is the IT8 target—IT8.7/1 for transmissive media, IT8.7/2 for reflective media—although there are others. Whichever target you use, you must have its accompanying reference file, which includes its unique measurement data. The profiling software will compare the data from the scan of the target to the reference file to make the profile.

Some profiling packages allow you to create your own reflective target by printing an image file of the target. The process is straightforward: first you print the target, then measure it to determine the color values, then you scan the target. The software uses your measured values as the reference file.

Preparing to Profile Your Scanner

Here are a few guidelines to keep in mind when scanning the target:

- Clean the target before scanning.
- Crop the target using the crop marks (see the example in the following exercise).

- Select a moderate resolution: 150 dpi will suffice; any more resolution is not necessary and will result in longer processing times. Use 16 bits if supported. A bit depth of 16 bits captures more color data for the profiling software to work with.

- Straighten the scan in Photoshop if necessary. If the scan is not straight, the profiling software will have difficulty finding the patches, resulting in profile errors.

- Don't adjust the resulting scan except to straighten it.

- Don't embed a profile in the resulting scan.

Here are some guidelines for creating good scanner profiles:

- Keep settings consistent: whatever settings you select to create the profile, use them to scan images. If your scanner software can save settings as presets, use this feature to ensure consistency.

- Turn off your scanner's automatic adjustment features. If you can't turn the automatic modes off, you'll have a hard time profiling the scanner.

   NOTE ▸ You can leave Applied Science Fiction's Digital ICE and GEM features alone—they don't affect color management.

- Turn off sharpening in the scanner, and sharpen in Photoshop.

- The easiest solution is to use the default scanner settings, which are often wide open, and edit in Photoshop.

- With some scanners you can use a display profile for onscreen previews. This improves the accuracy of the onscreen preview because it factors in the unique characteristics of your display—another reason to create a custom display profile!

   TIP ▸ If you send your images out to be scanned, ask the service bureau to embed the scanner profile in the saved image. If the service bureau staff will be editing the image for you, insist that they embed the Photoshop working-space profile in the saved file.

Using a Target to Create a Custom Scanner Profile

For the purpose of this exercise, we'll use GretagMacbeth ProfileMaker Professional and the accompanying sample scanner target. Other profile-creation suites include comparable functionality.

1 Launch ProfileMaker Professional. By default, it opens to the Monitor profiling tab.

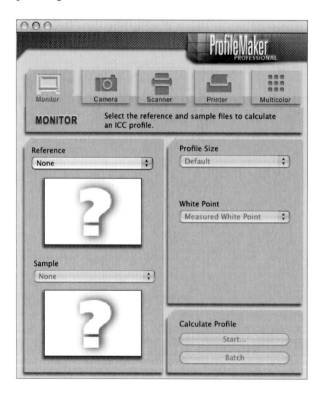

2   Click the Scanner button to begin. The Scanner profiling window opens.

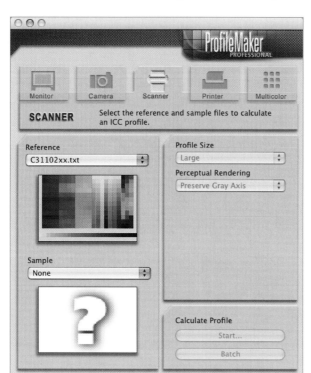

3   Choose C31102xx.txt from the Reference pop-up menu.

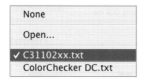

This tells ProfileMaker Professional which reference file to use in the profile creation. The reference file contains the known values for the corresponding target. ProfileMaker Professional provides support for different scanner target files, any of which can be used as long as you have the accompanying reference file. This exercise uses a sample reference file installed with ProfileMaker Professional.

4   Choose ExampleScan.tiff from the Sample pop-up menu.

The Sample selection is used to select the scan of the target. This exercise uses a sample scan installed with ProfileMaker Professional.

Once the scan is selected, a window automatically opens showing the scan of the target.

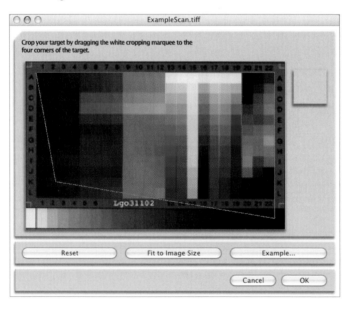

5   Crop the target by adjusting the marquee so that the selection includes
    only the color patches within the crop marks as well as the grayscale ramp
    at the bottom, as shown in the following image.

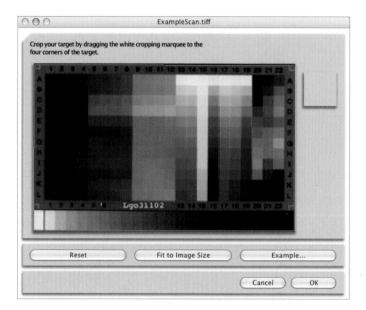

It's important to crop the image as described so that extraneous data does
not affect the profile creation. Click the Example button to see the exact
crop location. The Reset button will reset the marquee to the default settings, while the Fit to Image Size button will adjust the image of the target
to fit into the crop window.

6   Click OK to return to the Scanner tab of the main interface when you
    have adjusted all four corners. The Reference and Sample files should be
    selected, as shown in the following image.

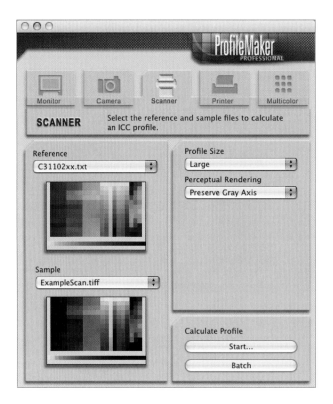

Two additional advanced options are provided: Profile Size and Perceptual Rendering. Profile Size enables you to change the size of the profile created. Large provides the best results in exchange for longer processing times. Select Large; with today's fast computers, there is a trivial difference in processing times between Large and other settings.

Perceptual Rendering factors the media and color characteristics of the device in such a way as to ensure that the human eye will perceive the image in the most faithful reproduction possible of the original. The recommended setting is Preserve Gray Axis.

ProfileMaker Professional is now ready to create the profile.

7   Click Start to create the profile.

8   Save the profile using a meaningful name such as the scanner name, the
    date the profile was created, and the media type. ProfileMaker Professional
    automatically selects the Profiles directory to save the profile in.

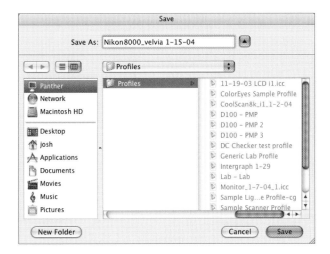

NOTE ▶ The trial version of ProfileMaker Professional included on this
book's CD does not save profiles.

9   Quit ProfileMaker Professional.

Creating Profiles for Output Devices

Creating a profile for your printer is the ultimate step in creating a color-
managed workflow. While it may seem like a daunting task, it's easier than it
seems, and it can have a profound impact on the effectiveness of your color
management system. Once you have an accurate printer profile, tasks like
soft-proofing (simulating your printer on your display) and press-proofing
(simulating a press on your printer) become not only possible but also invaluable.

Many printer manufacturers now include high-quality profiles for their devices in the box; some even include profiles for different paper and ink combinations. While these profiles are often quite accurate and will definitely make an improvement, they do not factor in variables such as subtle differences in ink and paper lots, changes that occur as a printer ages, and other environmental factors. They also don't help if you use third-party inks or papers, as even minor variations in paper noticeably affect how color is reproduced. For more accurate color management, creating a custom profile is the way to go.

To create printer profiles, a color-measurement device is used to measure patches printed from your printer. The device is controlled by the profiling software, which generates the profile by comparing the expected values with the actual values.

All profile-creation suites offer the capability to profile printers (many also include a suitable measurement device such as a spectrophotometer or colorimeter) in an easy-to-use package. The more expensive packages typically provide more advanced features (and increased complexity), such as greater control over the algorithm used to generate the profile, the capability to profile presses that use more than four colors, and profile editing (adjusting the profile after it has been created). If you need these types of advanced features, then evaluate packages such as GretagMacbeth ProfileMaker Professional or X-Rite's MonacoProfiler.

Preparing to Profile Your Printer
The fundamental process for creating a printer profile is relatively simple: You just print a target—or a set of color patches, which are typically included with the software—and measure it with a device. The software then generates a profile.

There are some important details to be aware of before starting:

- Determine whether your output device is CMYK or RGB. The profiling software will require you to print a target for one color space or the other. Most desktop printers are RGB, while most printing presses are CMYK. Desktop printers such as the Epson Stylus Photo and Canon photo printers are RGB, even though they use CMYK inks (the printer driver converts everything into RGB). If you're unsure whether your output device operates in CMYK or RGB, contact the manufacturer's technical support or use the exercise in Lesson 3 to find out before you create the profile.

- Calibrate your measurement device. As discussed in the beginning of this lesson, you will need an appropriate measurement device, such as the GretagMacbeth Eye-One Pro or X-Rite DTP41 spectrophotometer. Calibrating the device before profiling ensures that the device is measuring properly.

- Select the appropriate target. Most profiling applications include targets for different printers—at least for RGB and CMYK devices—and are designed to work well with a particular device. However, a number of targets are based on industry standards or are from known color gurus; these targets are often available for download on the Internet. They range in number and diversity of patches, layouts for specific devices, and page sizes. The target included with your software should suffice. If your profiling software supports different targets, try one with more patches to see if more data points improve the quality.

- Print the target properly. It is extremely important to follow the instructions for printing the target (provided with the profile-creation software), as there are specific steps required for printing the target, such as turning off the color management (compared with turning it on for normal printing) and setting the resolution and size.

Creating a Printer Profile

For the purpose of this exercise, we'll use GretagMacbeth ProfileMaker Professional. Other profile-creation suites include comparable functionality.

1   Launch ProfileMaker Professional. By default, it opens to the Monitor profiling tab.

2   Click the Printer button to begin. The Printer profiling window appears.

3   Chose the target reference file i1 RGB 1.5 Ref.txt from the Reference menu. This tells ProfileMaker Professional which target you will use to profile your printer.

ProfileMaker Professional includes a large number of targets and corresponding reference files, which provide support for different instruments, printer types, and target types. There are two important factors in selecting the target. First, determine whether your printer is RGB or CMYK; each supported target is labeled either RGB or CMYK.

NOTE ► Complete the exercise in Lesson 3 to determine your printer type.

Second, determine which measurement instrument you will use. ProfileMaker Professional includes targets preformatted for different instruments. For example, i1 RGB 1.5 Ref.txt is preformatted for the Eye-One device and for an RGB device, so it is the target we selected for this exercise.

Now that you've selected the target reference file according to the device and printer type, you will open and print the actual target.

4   Launch Photoshop by double-clicking its application name or icon in the Applications folder of your hard drive, or by clicking it in the Dock.

5   Choose File > Open and navigate to the Applications > ProfileMaker Pro 4.1.5 > Testcharts > EyeOne folder on your hard drive.

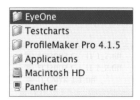

6   Choose the **i1 RGB 1.5.tiff** target and click Open.

7 If Photoshop presents the Missing Profile dialog, choose "Leave as is (don't color manage)." This tells Photoshop not to convert the file to a working space. Then click OK.

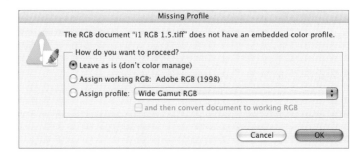

8 Ensure the file has opened correctly by checking the information area in the lower left of the image window. It should read Untagged RGB if you've opened the RGB target, or Untagged CMYK if you've opened the CMYK target. If so, skip to step 13.

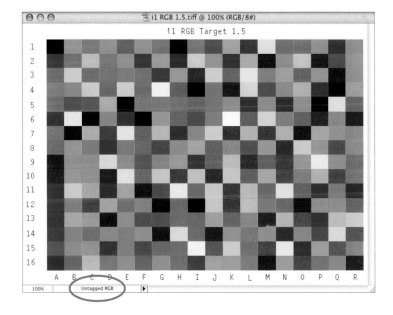

9 If the information area reads differently, choose Document Profile from the pop-up menu.

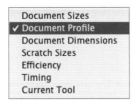

10 If the pop-up menu says Document Profile but the information area still doesn't say Untagged RGB/CMYK, choose Image > Mode > Assign Profile.

11 In the Assign Profile dialog box, choose Don't Color Manage This Document and click OK.

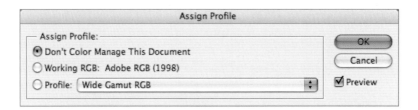

12 Check the information area again, choosing Document Profile from the pop-up menu if necessary, and it should read Untagged RGB or Untagged CMYK.

Now we can print the target.

13 Choose File > Print with Preview.

14 In the Print dialog, check the Show More Options box and choose Color Management from the pop-up menu just below it.

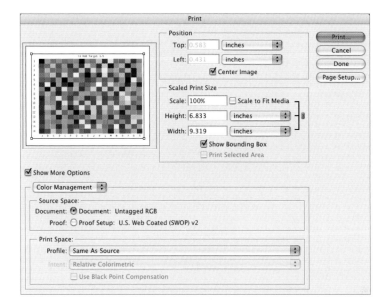

15 Under Source Space, choose Document: Untagged RGB, and under Print Space, choose Same As Source from the Profile pop-up menu. As in previous exercises, we're telling Photoshop not to color manage the file but rather to send it straight to the printer. The goal is to capture the printer's native gamut. Applying any color management will affect the results.

16 Click Print, and in the printer driver dialog that appears, choose your printer from the Printer pop-up menu.

17 Click the Copies & Pages pop-up menu to locate your printer's media settings, and then choose the correct paper for your device. The location of the media option varies with each printer; look for it under a heading such as Print Settings, as shown in the following figure. This is an essential step, as the media option controls the amount of ink the printer will use. If the paper you're using is not listed, either check with the paper manufacturer or choose the closest available setting. If you have the option, disable any automatic settings (such as by selecting Advanced Settings, also shown in the following figure).

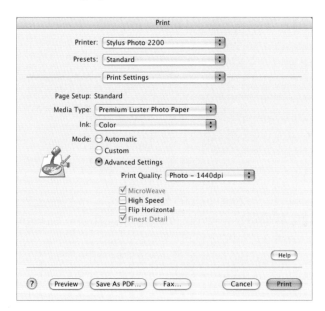

18 Click the Copies & Pages pop-up menu again to locate your printer's color-management options, and *turn them off.* The location of these options varies with each printer; look for them under a heading such as Custom, Advanced, or Color Management. The following image shows the Color Management option in the Epson Stylus Photo 2200 printer driver, with No Color Adjustment selected.

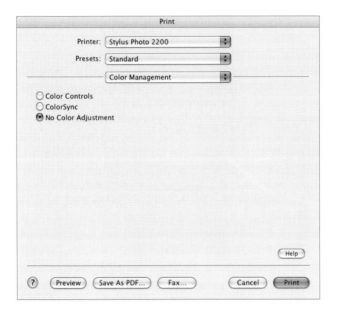

TIP Save these printer settings to use again when printing with the profile. It's important to always print with the same settings—changing the resolution or paper type will affect the results. Save them by choosing Save As from the Presets menu.

19 Click Print to start printing the target.

20 Once you have successfully printed the target, return to ProfileMaker Professional to begin measuring the printed target.

21 Select Open from the Sample menu. Navigate to the Color Management in Mac OS X Book Files > Lessons > Lesson04 folder on your hard drive and select the **Stylus_Photo_2200_i1.txt** file.

This file contains measurement data for the Epson Stylus Photo 2200 with the i1 target. At this stage, you would normally use your instrument to measure the printed target. Instead of selecting a file containing the measurement data, you would select a device from the Sample list. Selecting a device from the list enables ProfileMaker Professional to communicate with the instrument directly.

TIP ▶ Wait until the target is dry before measuring it.

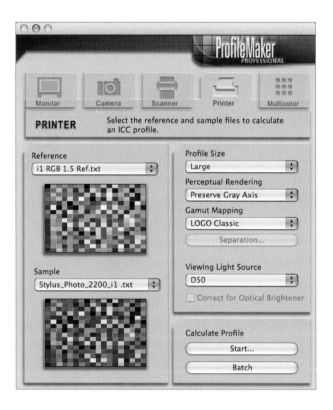

Several options affect how the profile is created. Profile Size and Perceptual Rendering were discussed in the previous exercise. Gamut Mapping describes how out-of-gamut colors are adjusted so that they are in gamut. ProfileMaker Professional provides two methods: LOGO Classic (which I selected) or LOGO Chroma Plus. Either one is a good choice.

The Viewing Light Source option should be set to the color temperature of the lights under which you will view images. For example, if you have a light box, select the color temperature that corresponds to your light box. If you will use ambient lighting to view images, select D65. The best method to determine the correct setting for Viewing Light Source, aside from using a light booth, is to experiment with different settings and compare the results with the display.

22 Click Start to create the profile. ProfileMaker Professional will prompt you to name the profile. Again, use a meaningful name: for example, the printer name, paper type, and date it was created.

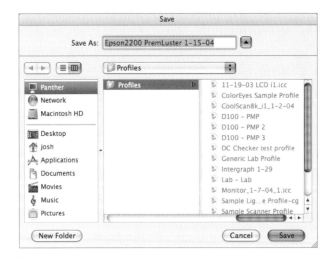

NOTE ▸ The trial version of ProfileMaker Professional included on this book's CD does not save profiles.

23 Click Save. ProfileMaker Professional will process the data and create the profile. It will take several minutes to create the profile, during which time ProfileMaker Professional displays a progress bar.

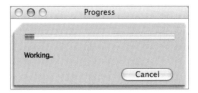

24 When ProfileMaker Professional is finished, choose File > Quit.

Comparing Output Profiles

Once you've created a custom printer profile, you can easily compare it with the generic profile for your printer, similar to the way you compared your display profiles earlier in this lesson. This exercise will show you how to do that, which will illustrate the value of creating a custom profile for your printer.

1 Launch the ColorSync Utility inside the Applications > Utilities folder on your hard drive.

2 Click the Profiles icon.

On the left, the utility displays a list of all of the profiles installed on your system, organized by category. If your screen looks different, click the triangle on the Profile list box and select "Group by class" to change the view.

3 Choose a generic profile for your printer from the list, such as SP200 Premium Luster_PK. Information on the selected profile, including a 3D color model, is displayed on the right.

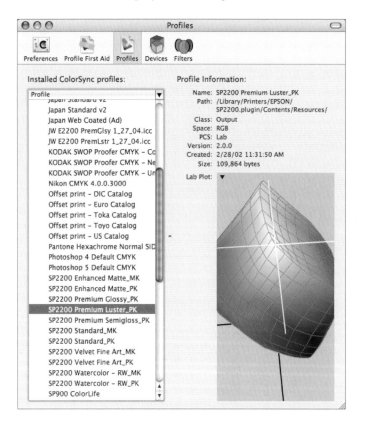

Notice the location, color space, creation date, size, and other information for this profile, including its Lab Plot 3D visual representation.

4   Click the triangle in the Lab Plot area and choose "Hold for comparison" from the pop-up menu.

5   Choose a profile for your printer such as JW E2200 PremLstr 1_27_04 from the left-hand list. The ColorSync Utility displays an overlay plot of the two profiles.

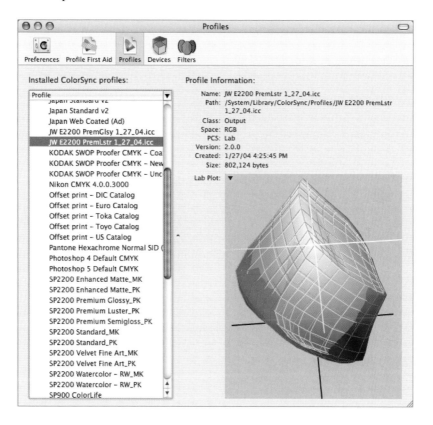

The ghosted white outline is the first profile, the generic Stylus 2200 profile, compared to the profile created for me by Chromix. The areas on the outside of the cube, in color, and the dark section crosscutting the cube are areas where the custom profile contains more data than the generic Epson profile. The custom profile's larger color gamut can be attributed to a number of factors: differences in the ink or paper, a newer printer driver that is affecting the output of the printer, or variables in the profiling device and software.

The custom profile's larger color gamut, however, doesn't ensure that it will yield better, more accurate, or more predictable color output. The only sure way to determine which profile provides the best results is to visually compare the results of each profile both onscreen and in print. Once your system is fully profiled and your applications are set up, print an image using each profile, and then compare the results, both between the profiles and with what you see onscreen (an exercise you'll complete in Lesson 6).

You can also use the preceding exercise to compare other, disparate profiles: your display profile to your printer profile, for example. That will illustrate the differences in the devices, and you will get a much better picture of the differences by running the comparison yourself; the figure in step 5 on the preceding page shows only one angle of the three-dimensional color gamut. As you rotate the color model, you will see areas of color that do not overlap.

Try this exercise with profiles for your devices, as well as standard press profiles such as U.S. Sheetfed Coated v2.

Profiling Printing Presses

With desktop printers, you can control the device and you are typically making a few prints at a time. With a printing press, in contrast, you typically have no control and are making a lot of prints. Due to the expensive nature of printing on press, color becomes even more critical. You can still take advantage of color management if the final destination for your color work is a printing press, but since you will have less control over the process, you will need to work with your printing partner to determine how to best handle color management.

Most printing companies utilize process control to keep their presses printing consistently, often to one of several printing industry standards (based on the specific process, paper type, etc.). The ideal situation is to find a printer that understands color management and has custom ICC profiles to which they keep their press(es) calibrated. Many printers will have instructions for using these profiles in conjunction with their services. Lesson 9 will cover the use of profiles to proof and separate your color documents in more detail.

An important issue to keep in mind with traditional offset printing is that—from the moment you hand your color data to the printer to the time the job comes off the press—getting your document printed introduces several steps, each of which has its own variables that can affect the final color. Your document may be output to color-separation films, which are then used to make the plates for the press. The printer will likely insist that a proof be made (often called a contract proof). Since the printer will agree to match this proof (hence the term *contract proof*), it's important to carefully check the film proofs and make changes based on how they look. The press plates will be made from the same color data as the proof.

Digital presses reduce the variability (and cost) of offset printing by eliminating the need for films and plates. Most digital press operators will still offer a proof, although it will typically be from a desktop printer (such as a high-quality inkjet printer) using profiles that simulate the press. You can also use your desktop printer to simulate the press (a technique covered in Lesson 9). Regardless of the type of press, it's a good idea to give your proof to the printer.

Finally, you'll want to insist on a press check to ensure the prints coming off the press match the contract proof.

If your printer doesn't offer ICC press profiles, you have a few choices:

1   Use standard press profiles (such as SWOP) to proof and separate your images. Then communicate with your printer—let the printer know what type of press profile or standard you used to separate your images. Be sure to use a contract proof. Press profiles are widely available, and applications such as Photoshop typically include several standard press profiles.

2   Find a new printer who offers ICC profiles and keeps its presses well calibrated.

3   Create the press profile yourself, although this is not highly recommended unless you operate your own press. It will be expensive, but if you're doing enough printing with that printer, it can be worth it. The process is essentially the same as the exercises included in this lesson, except the choice of target will be different. You'll want a CMYK target, such as the one included with ProfileMaker Professional.

The most important point in creating or obtaining press profiles is to communicate with your printer about the process.

What You've Learned

- You can create display profiles in three ways: using visual calibration, using a display calibrator, or using a calibrated display system.

- Digital cameras can be profiled with third-party software, but variables such as lighting must be controlled for the profile to be useful.

- Creating scanner profiles requires reference targets based on the film and emulsion type of the originals. All internal color management and automatic color settings should be shut off to avoid unintended results.

- Printing a target for printer profiling requires all color management to be turned off to ensure that the target is accurate.

- The Apple ColorSync Utility enables you to compare profiles and to see a visual representation of the profile's color gamut.

5

Lesson Files   Color Management in Mac OS X Book Files > Lessons > Lesson05

Time   This lesson takes approximately 2 hours to complete.

Goals   Set up Photoshop's Color Settings for a color-managed workflow

Configure scanners for acquiring color-managed images

Create a color-managed digital camera workflow

Convert RAW camera images using color management

Color Managing Images

To implement color management in design and production processes, you need to understand how applications are configured to handle color data, where color data comes from, when the color data is converted from one space to the next, how data is tagged to ensure the accurate communication of color intent, and who is responsible for guaranteeing the accuracy and quality of the data.

Addressing all of these issues for your particular design and production function will ensure the consistent and repeatable handling of color—which will ultimately reduce the time and money you spend on producing color images, art, and documents.

This lesson explores how to implement color management at the point when photographic images are brought into the process—how to configure Adobe Photoshop's color-management settings, how to import and color manage scanned images, and how to import and color manage images from digital cameras—so that they can be used in page assembly, soft-proofed, and ultimately printed.

Adobe Photoshop: The Starting Point

Adobe Photoshop is where you perform most, if not all, color manipulation, including correction, separation, printing, and proofing. Adobe has fine-tuned the color-management implementation in Photoshop over the years, and versions 7 and CS provide comprehensive color-management features. In this lesson, we will explore them. The first step is to set up Photoshop's preferences so that it understands how you want to handle color data.

Configuring Photoshop's Color Settings

Photoshop centralizes all of its color-management preferences in the Color Settings dialog. These settings control how Photoshop handles color data and how it interacts with other color management systems and devices. Therefore, it's extremely important to configure these settings correctly for your production requirements. We'll do that now in the current version of the software, Adobe Photoshop CS.

1   Launch Adobe Photoshop and choose Photoshop > Color Settings.

2   In the Color Settings dialog that appears, check the Advanced Mode box.

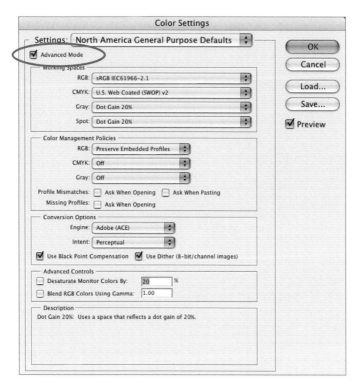

Photoshop's Color Settings enables you to select from a set of predefined color-management options or to customize settings for your particular workflow. The Advanced Mode provides additional options for professional color-management settings, including choices for working-space profiles.

3   Move your cursor over the various pop-up menus and options in the Color Settings dialog. Notice that Photoshop displays context-sensitive explanations of each option in the Description field at the bottom of the dialog. These will help you decide which options are best for your workflow.

4 Click and hold the Settings pop-up menu.

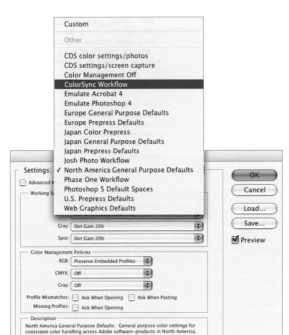

The Settings menu shows the various predefined color-management settings for common workflows that are supported by Photoshop. When you choose one of these presets, the various Working Spaces (RGB, CMYK, Gray space, and Spot color profiles), Color Management Policies (color-conversion options), and other options in the Color Settings dialog change accordingly.

Most of the presets are designed for the prepress workflows of various geographic regions and use the appropriate profiles for those printing processes. For example, selecting Japan Prepress Defaults automatically selects a CMYK profile for typical Japanese printing processes. We'll get into the specifics of configuring these settings in a few steps; first, let's explore some of the presets.

5   Choose Settings > Color Management Off.

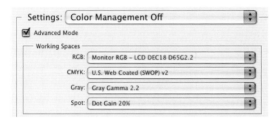

The Color Management Off setting is a bit misleading, as you can't actually turn off color management in Photoshop. This setting tells Photoshop to function like an application that does not support color management. It ignores embedded profiles and does not embed profiles when images are saved. This setting essentially assumes that every image uses the same working space as the one set in the Working Spaces settings.

6   Choose Settings > Web Graphics Defaults.

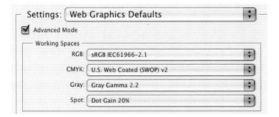

Web Graphics Defaults is essentially the same as Color Management Off, except that sRGB is selected as the RGB working space. sRGB is a display profile that, like Adobe RGB (1998), can be used as an RGB working-space profile. Microsoft and HP, its creators, based it on what those companies believed was the average PC's display gamut, a relatively small color space. Small color spaces do not make good working spaces.

7 Choose Settings > ColorSync Workflow.

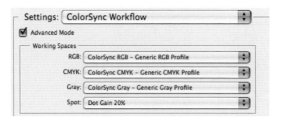

ColorSync Workflow uses the color-management preferences specified in the ColorSync Utility, which we configured in Lesson 1, for the Working Spaces profiles. The ColorSync Workflow preset also selects the Apple CMM as the conversion engine.

ColorSync Workflow is a good choice if you use a mix of Adobe and non-Adobe applications. However, if you work in a cross-platform environment, you will want to use the same settings across both Mac OS and Windows and therefore would not want to use ColorSync Workflow.

TIP ▶ If you'd like to interactively see the effects of these settings, click the Cancel button, open an image in Photoshop, and then return to the Color Settings dialog. Then check the Preview box under the Save button. When the Preview box is checked, Photoshop shows the effect of each setting on the open image file.

Adobe's presets provide a good starting point for color-managed work-flows, but customizing them for your particular environment will provide maximum benefit. Let's customize the ColorSync Workflow option as a way to learn about all of the specific options and how to choose what's best for you.

8 In the Working Spaces section, choose RGB > Adobe RGB (1998).

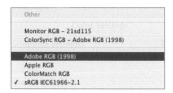

Notice that the Settings pop-up menu changes from ColorSync Workflow to Custom.

This is a good time to explore the concept of working spaces. The basic color-management premise in Photoshop is that each open file can be in a different *working space*. A working space is the color space in which you edit the file, and it can be different from the original color space of the file, which is called the *document* color space. Adobe has also separated the document working space from the display space, which means that the definition of RGB is not specifically tied to the current display's color space.

Working spaces are based either on color-space profiles such as Adobe RGB or on device profiles. Color-space profiles are device independent, which means that the color onscreen is independent of your display gamut. This makes them a good choice for working spaces. A device profile is meant specifically for the device on which it is based. Using a device profile as a working space essentially means that you are restricting your working space to the colors that can be reproduced by the device upon which the profile is based.

When you select working-space profiles in Color Settings, you are telling Photoshop which working space to use when opening an image without an embedded profile, as well as which profile to use when performing a color-mode change (for example, from RGB to CMYK).

The working space is also used when displaying an image onscreen. Photoshop determines the display profile from the ColorSync Preferences. When the image is displayed onscreen, Photoshop converts the color data from the working space to the display profile to ensure that what you are seeing is accurate. Photoshop does not actually change the data in the file.

When choosing an RGB working-space profile, you want to select a space larger than the gamut of your devices—but not too large. When you edit images, you have a limited number of color values to work with. If you select a space that is too large, the distance between values may be too far apart, and those differences could lead to banding or other distortions in the displayed images.

Photoshop provides several RGB working-space options. Among them are the following:

▶ Monitor RGB — *display profile name* — uses the display profile as your RGB working space.

▶ ColorSync — *default profile* — uses the default RGB profile set in the ColorSync Preferences.

▶ Adobe RGB (1998), which we have selected — is a working space developed by Adobe. It is designed to provide the best working space for print production. The gamuts of most imaging devices, including CMYK printing processes, fit into the Adobe RGB (1998) gamut.

▶ Apple RGB — is designed to emulate how Photoshop 4.0 and earlier versions handle color. The only reason to use it is if you are trying to match how an image looked under one of these older versions of Photoshop.

▶ ColorMatch RGB — is based on the color space of the older Radius PressView monitors. Unless you are using a PressView or trying to emulate PressView conditions, there is no compelling reason to use this as your working space.

▶ sRGB — is designed to represent the average PC monitor, and while it is suitable for Web graphics, it is not recommended for print production.

NOTE ▶ When the Advanced Mode box is checked, Photoshop lists all of the installed profiles on your computer, both device and working space, in the working-spaces menus. It also provides a Custom RGB option that allows you to create your own RGB working space, which you can in turn save and load using the appropriate commands.

9 Choose CMYK > U.S. Web Coated (SWOP) v2.

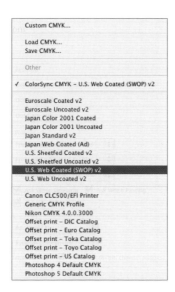

CMYK working spaces are essentially printing processes characterized by various ink-and-paper combinations, dot-gain settings, and separation options such as ink limits.

If you have a custom press profile, you would select it as your CMYK working space. When you perform a mode change to or from CMYK, Photoshop will use the CMYK working-space profile for the conversion. It will also use the CMYK working-space profile when you open a CMYK image that lacks an embedded profile.

If you need to convert images to CMYK but do not have a custom press profile, and one is not available from your printer, select one of the profiles provided by Adobe, basing it on the type of printing process and paper that will be used, such as U.S. Web Coated (SWOP) v2.

As with RGB working spaces, Photoshop provides the ability to create custom CMYK working-space profiles. This is useful if your print provider does not have a profile but can tell you what separation settings to use when converting your images to CMYK.

NOTE ▶ If you edit a document in Lab mode, Photoshop will convert the image to the display color space. You cannot select a Lab profile as a working space.

10 Choose Gray > Gray Gamma 1.8.

The Gray working space provides a default setting for grayscale images. The setting Gray Gamma 1.8 uses the grayscale equivalent of the default grayscale gamma of Mac OS X displays; Gray Gamma 2.2 matches the default grayscale display of Windows computers. (Remember, the gamma of a monitor defines the overall contrast of midtones.) Alternatively, you can define the Gray working space in terms of dot gain. If you want to do so, check with your print provider for the appropriate selection.

NOTE ▶ The Spot working-space pop-up menu provides a setting for spot colors, such as Pantone colors, that may be used in the printing process. We will leave this setting unchanged for now.

11 In the Color Management Policies section, make sure RGB > Preserve Embedded Profiles is chosen.

Color Management Policies determines how Photoshop handles images whose document spaces differ from the working spaces we just set. Two types of exceptions may occur: profile mismatches and missing profiles. When an image contains an embedded profile different from the current working space, there is a profile mismatch; when an image lacks an embedded profile altogether, there is a missing profile. You can instruct Photoshop to respond to these exceptions by choosing from the following three options:

▶ Off — tells Photoshop to disregard embedded profile mismatches and to use the Working Spaces setting. For images without embedded profiles, the document will remain untagged.

▶ Preserve Embedded Profiles — uses the embedded profile as the working space. This is the preferred option, and we have chosen it.

NOTE ▶ Preserve Embedded Profiles is also already chosen in the Color Management Policies' CMYK and Gray pop-up menus, as part of the ColorSync Workflow preset, which we are editing. We will leave those options as is.

▶ Convert to Working RGB, Convert to Working CMYK, or Convert to Working Gray — converts all images from the embedded profile to the profile chosen in the Working Spaces section of the Color Settings dialog.

These actions work in conjunction with an additional set of options, the Profile Mismatches and Missing Profiles check boxes.

12 Confirm that Ask When Opening and Ask When Pasting are checked under Profile Mismatches, and that Ask When Opening is checked under Missing Profiles.

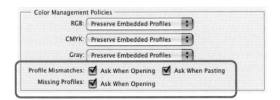

When enabled, these settings tell Photoshop to ask you if you want to override the default action each time a profile mismatch or missing profile is encountered, essentially ignoring the policy setting. When these settings are disabled, Photoshop warns you that a profile mismatch or missing profile has been encountered, but only provides you with the action as set in the policy.

With these boxes checked and the RGB, CMYK, and Gray policies set to Preserve Embedded Profiles, Photoshop will do the following:

▶   Tag new documents created in Photoshop with the default working-space profile.

▶   Open images tagged with the working-space profile without changes.

▶   Display an Embedded Profile Mismatch dialog, as shown in the following image, when you open an image tagged with a profile other than the working-space profile. This dialog will ask you how to handle the data, and the "Use the embedded profile" option will be selected by default (as a result of our policy settings). When you encounter this dialog, click OK to open the document and edit the image in the document space—unless the document space is a scanner or camera profile. Those color spaces are not appropriate to edit in.

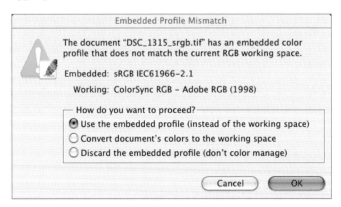

▶   Edit images without a profile in the specified Photoshop working space, but will not tag the image with a profile.

Essentially, you want to always keep images in their document spaces for editing. So if the file is tagged with a profile, use it and do not convert to a working-space profile. Rarely is there an advantage to converting a file to another working space. If the working space is larger than the document space, nothing is gained; you usually don't get more color data. However, if the working space is smaller than the document space, you typically do lose data.

There are only a couple of situations in which you will want to convert an image to a different working space. First, if the image does not have an embedded profile and you do not know its source, then you should tag it with the working-space profile. Second, if you are compositing multiple images together, you want all of your images to be in the same working space, and you may need to convert some images to achieve this.

We will see how these policy settings work later in the lesson, when we open images from different sources. Right now, let's look at the additional options enabled in the Advanced Mode of the Color Settings dialog.

Configuring Advanced Color Controls

As you saw in the previous exercise, the Advanced Mode of the Color Settings dialog allows you to select any profile as a working space as long as the profile is in the same color space as the working space. In addition, the Advanced Mode enables two other sets of options: Conversion Options and Advanced Controls.

1   In the Conversion Options area, choose Engine > Apple CMM.

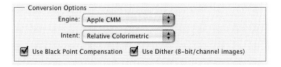

Photoshop lets you choose from at least three CMMs, which Adobe calls *conversion engines,* to convert colors between different profiles. They are as follows:

▶   Adobe (ACE), which stands for Adobe Color Engine — is Adobe's own CMM. It is built into all Adobe professional design applications but is unavailable to non-Adobe applications.

▶   Apple ColorSync — tells Photoshop to use the CMM specified by the ColorSync Preferences. If Automatic is selected as the Preferred CMM in the ColorSync Preferences, ColorSync will use the Apple CMM unless a profile contains a specific instruction to use a different CMM.

▶   Apple CMM — tells Photoshop to use Apple's own CMM, disregarding any specific instructions that may be contained in a profile.

If you work in an environment that uses a mix of Adobe and non-Adobe applications, choose the Apple CMM conversion option to ensure consistent results across applications. This option is better than the Apple ColorSync option, which can be overridden by specific instructions contained in a profile.

If you work in an all-Adobe but cross-platform environment, choose Adobe (ACE) to ensure consistency across platforms. If you work in an all-Adobe, all-Mac environment, you can choose either Adobe ACE or Apple CMM, as you will have access to both conversion options in all of the professional Adobe products you may use. If you work with applications that include their own CMMs and profiles, select Apple ColorSync.

2   Make sure that Relative Colorimetric is chosen from the Intent pop-up menu.

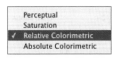

As explained in Lesson 1, the rendering intent controls how color is mapped between the gamuts of two profiles. This menu lets you choose which rendering intent Photoshop will use to convert an image upon opening, to make color-mode changes, and to display color values in the Info palette. Relative Colorimetric, chosen by the ColorSync Workflow preset, compares the highlight of the source color space to that of the destination color space and shifts out-of-gamut colors to the closest reproducible color in the destination color space. Relative Colorimetric is a good choice when the majority of colors are in gamut. For an image that contains many out-of-gamut colors, Perceptual is a good choice, because it preserves the overall relationship between colors.

NOTE ▶ We'll learn how to check an image for out-of-gamut colors in Lesson 6.

3   Make sure that Use Black Point Compensation and Use Dither (8-bit/channel images) are both checked.

Checking Use Black Point Compensation compensates for differences in the black points of two profiles. Although the effect is difficult to detect, it's a good idea to check this option.

Checking Use Dither is also a good idea because it can reduce banding that may appear when an image is converted between two color spaces.

4   In the Advanced Controls area, make sure Desaturate Monitor Colors By and Blend RGB Colors Using Gamma are both unchecked.

Desaturate Monitor Colors is designed to accommodate very large working spaces, and checking it can lead to onscreen colors that do not match printed colors. Blend RGB Colors, meanwhile, allows you to choose a gamma when overlaying two colors. When it is disabled, RGB colors are blended in the document color space, which is how most applications perform this task.

Now that you have customized Photoshop's Color Settings for your workflow and production environment, you can save the settings so that they can be easily restored if they are ever changed, and so that you can share them with other users and among other Adobe applications.

5 Click the Save button. Photoshop displays the Save dialog.

6 Enter an intuitive filename in the Save As field, and click Save.

7 When the Color Settings Comment dialog appears, enter a description for your Color Settings file if you'd like, and click OK.

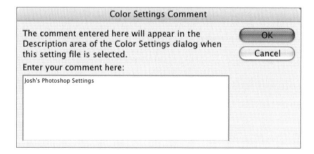

Congratulations! You have now configured Photoshop to work in a color-managed workflow. Photoshop will use these custom Color Settings to determine how to open and display images, ensuring that they are being reproduced as accurately as possible. In addition, because Adobe Creative Suite applications such as InDesign, Illustrator, and Acrobat all use the same Color Settings preferences, you can load your saved settings file into each of those applications, an exercise we'll perform in Lesson 7. This will ensure consistency across all of those applications without your having to manually re-create the settings.

Importing Images Using Apple Image Capture

If your scanner or digital camera supports the Apple Image Capture architecture, you can use the Image Capture application to bring photographic images into your workflow with color management. Image Capture also works with scanners that support TWAIN, an industry-standard format for scanner drivers, as well as all currently shipping Epson scanners.

Image Capture attempts to provide an automatic color-management workflow for scanned or digitally photographed images. The process begins when you first plug the scanner or camera into your Mac: ColorSync looks for an ICC profile in the device driver. If one is available, ColorSync will use that profile as the source color space for the image. If one is not available, ColorSync will use a generic device profile. If you have a custom profile for your scanner or camera, you can tell ColorSync to use it rather than the profile that is automatically selected.

Once a profile is assigned to the device, Image Capture will use the profile in two ways. First, it will perform an on-the-fly color transformation from the device profile to the display profile when it displays the image onscreen. It will also automatically embed the device profile in the image when the file is saved. When the image is opened in Photoshop (or another image-editing program that supports color management), Photoshop will recognize the profile (more on that shortly).

Here's how to use Apple Image Capture to capture color-managed TIF or JPEG images from a digital camera.

1   Launch Image Capture by double-clicking its application name or icon in the Applications folder of your hard drive, or by clicking it in the Dock.

2   Choose Image Capture > Preferences.

3   In the Camera panel of the Image Capture Preferences dialog that appears, click the "When a camera is connected, open:" pop-up menu and choose Image Capture, and then click OK to close the dialog.

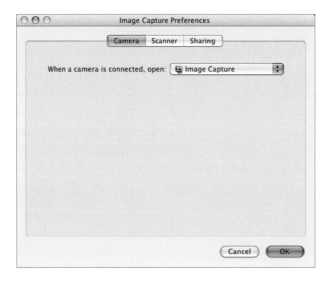

4   Plug your digital camera into your Mac.

When Mac OS X recognizes that a camera has been connected, it automatically launches Image Capture and prompts you to download images from the camera, as shown in the following figure.

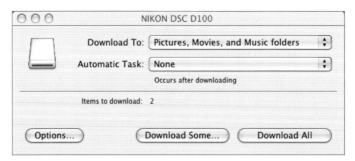

5   Click the Options button.

6   In the Image Capture Options dialog that appears, click the Download Options button.

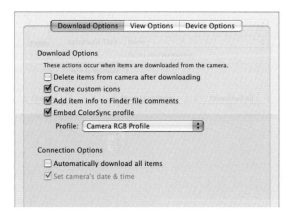

7   If you have a custom profile for your camera, choose it from the Profile pop-up menu. Otherwise, choose a working space profile such as Adobe RGB (1998). The chosen profile will be embedded in the image when it is downloaded to your Mac.

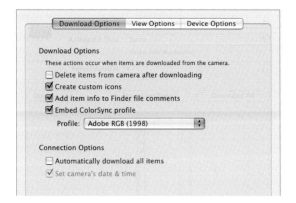

8   If your camera embeds a profile in images, uncheck the Embed ColorSync profile box. Otherwise, Image Capture will overwrite the embedded profile when it copies the image to the Mac.

   NOTE ▶ Image Capture doesn't support embedding profiles in RAW files.

9   Click OK to close the Options dialog.

10   Click Download All to begin downloading your camera's images to your Mac. Once the download is complete, you can open the images in Adobe Photoshop for editing and printing.

>   **NOTE** ▶ If the profile embedded in the image is different than Photoshop's RGB working space profile), the Photoshop Embedded Profile Mismatch dialog will appear when you open the file; select the "Convert document's colors to the working space" option, and then click OK.

Color Managing Scanned Images

How to color manage scanned images in your production process depends largely on the type of software you use to control your scanner. You can import and color manage scanned images in three basic ways:

*   Using the Apple Image Capture application
*   Using a stand-alone scanning application that comes with your scanner
*   Using a Photoshop or TWAIN-compatible plug-in

>   **NOTE** ▶ In all cases, these workflow options presume your software supports ICC color management.

Scanning with Stand-alone Scanner Software

Most professional-quality scanners include their own software that provides a dedicated interface to the scanner. This software controls not only the tonal reproduction of the image but also the color. When working with scanned images, you make adjustments based on the colors you see onscreen. Without color management, what you see onscreen is not necessarily an accurate representation of the scanned data, making it unreliable to use as a basis for adjustments.

With color-managed scanned images, you can have confidence in their onscreen representation. You can also be confident that the image will be properly reproduced from within other applications—as long as they, too, support color management. This is particularly important if other people work with your images.

The following exercise demonstrates how to configure a stand-alone scanning application to support a color-managed workflow. It uses Nikon Scan 4, which can be downloaded at www.nikonusa.com. If you use different scanning software, look for comparable commands and functions in that application.

1   Launch Nikon Scan 4, which is located in the Applications folder on your hard drive.

The first time Nikon Scan runs, it presents the Color Space Wizard, as shown in the following figure.

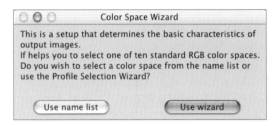

2   Click "Use name list."

Nikon Scan supports a full color-management workflow, including support for working spaces, display correction, and profile embedding.

3   In the RGB Profile List dialog, select Adobe RGB (1998).

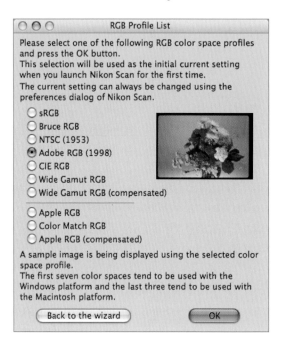

This setting determines the working-space profile that Nikon Scan will use. Much like Photoshop, Nikon Scan uses this profile as the editing space for the image. By selecting the same working space as you did in Photoshop, the image will look the same when displayed in Nikon Scan and in Photoshop.

NOTE ▶ If you chose a different RGB working space in Photoshop, then choose that one in your scanning software.

4   Click OK.

5   Choose Nikon Scan 4 > Preferences.

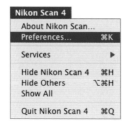

6   Select Color Management from the left-hand list. Ensure that "Use Nikon Color Management System" is checked, and then click the Monitor button and select "Use factory default monitor profile."

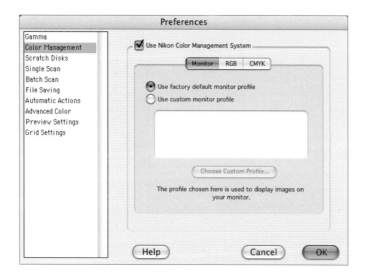

Nikon Scan uses a display profile for onscreen previews. By selecting "Use factory default monitor profile" you're telling it to use the default profile set in ColorSync. Alternatively, you could tell it to use a custom profile.

7 Click the RGB button. Adobe RGB (1998) is listed as the "Color space" profile because we selected it in step 3.

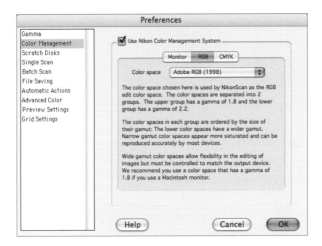

Nikon Scan uses the same approach as Photoshop for working spaces. When the image is scanned, it is converted from the native color space of the scanner to the selected working-space profile. The display profile is used to interpret the colors for display.

8 Click the CMYK button and make sure "Use factory default CMYK profile" is selected.

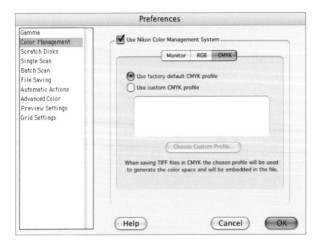

The CMYK setting determines the working space that Nikon Scan uses to convert scanned images to the CMYK color space. The "Use factory default CMYK profile" setting instructs Nikon Scan to use the CMYK default profile set in the ColorSync Preferences. This is the preferred setting; even if you are using a custom CMYK profile, it is better to set this as the default setting in ColorSync so that all ColorSync-aware applications are set to use it as the default. If you use a specific CMYK profile for separations, however, you would select that profile as the CMYK profile.

TIP ▶ If you need to deliver CMYK files to a client or print provider, it's better to scan images into RGB and save them, and then convert your master RGB file to CMYK. This approach allows you to separate images into CMYK for different printers without losing quality.

9   Click OK and quit Nikon Scan. Now when the software saves a scanned image, it will automatically embed the working-space profile into the image.

NOTE ▶ Some stand-alone scanner applications do not support working-space profiles but do embed a scanner profile in the image file. In this case, you will want to use Photoshop to convert to the working-space profile. Scanner color spaces do not make good editing spaces.

Scanning with Plug-in Scanner Software

Unlike stand-alone scanner applications, plug-in scanner tools work from within other applications, such as Adobe Photoshop. As with configuring stand-alone scanner software for color management, the important thing with plug-in scanning tools is to use the same working-space profile as Photoshop does. This ensures that the onscreen preview in the plug-in will match the image in Photoshop.

The following exercise demonstrates how to configure a plug-in scanning application to support a color-managed workflow. As in the previous exercise, it uses Nikon Scan 4, which has a plug-in mode. Again, Nikon Scan 4 can be downloaded at www.nikonusa.com. If you use a different scanner plug-in, look for comparable commands and functions in that tool.

1   Launch Adobe Photoshop and choose File > Import > Nikon Scan 4.

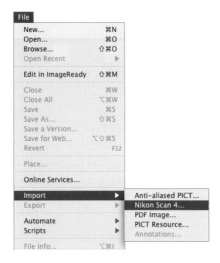

2   In the Nikon Scan plug-in window, click the Prefs button.

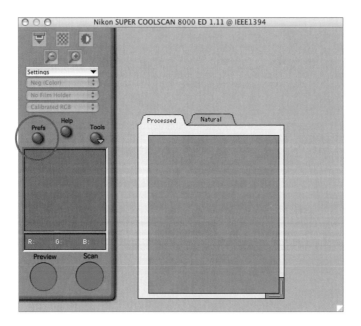

The Preferences dialog appears.

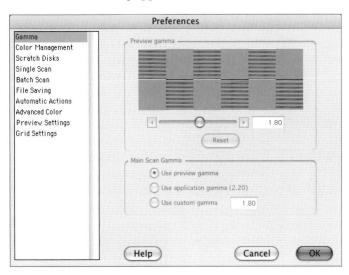

3   Click Color Management in the left-hand list.

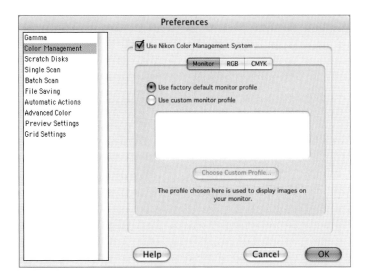

4   Configure the color-management settings as described in steps 6 through 9 of the previous exercise.

When you're finished, the Nikon Scan plug-in preview and the image in Photoshop should match.

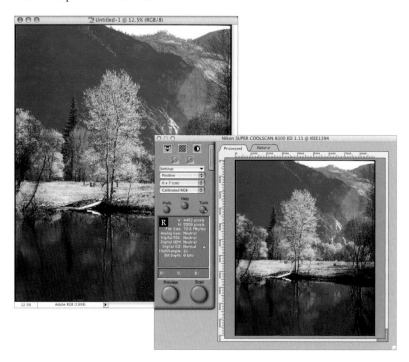

5   Close the Nikon Scan plug-in.

Scanning Without Color-Management Support

If your scanner doesn't support the Apple Image Capture API or color management, you can still use it in a color-managed workflow. The best approach is:

1   Create a custom scanner profile as described in Lesson 4.

2   Scan the image. Keep in mind that the onscreen preview will not be an accurate color representation of the image. Consider scanning with the scanner's curves settings wide open.

3   Open the image in Photoshop and convert it to the RGB working space, using the custom scanner profile as the source space.

4   Save the image with the working-space profile embedded.

Importing JPEG and TIFF Digital Camera Images

Working with files from digital cameras presents more options than working with scanned images. Digital cameras, particularly higher-end single-lens reflex models, can provide files in a standard format such as JPEG or TIFF, as well as in a proprietary RAW format. Each option has its own advantages and color-management workflow. Let's first explore workflows for cameras that support the capture of standard file-format JPEG and TIFF images. There are three options for importing standard file-format images:

• Use profiles embedded by the camera

• Use custom camera profiles

• Import images from digital cameras without color-management support

Importing Images with Embedded Working-Space Profiles

Some cameras support the use of working-space profiles. The camera converts the image from the camera's native color space to the working-space profile selected in the camera's preferences, and then embeds the profile in the image.

The most commonly supported in-camera working-space profiles are Adobe RGB (1998) and sRGB. Adobe RGB (1998) provides the best option for a print-production color workflow, both for desktop photo printers and printing presses. sRGB, which is a much smaller color space, is a more suitable work-flow for Web graphics. If you deliver your work both in a print format and to the Web, use Adobe RGB (1998) and convert the images to sRGB when you save them for the Web.

If you use Adobe RGB (1998) in your camera and as the Photoshop RGB working-space profile, then you can open the image in Photoshop without any conversion. If you have a different working-space profile either in the camera or in Photoshop, you use the embedded profile upon opening.

1   Launch Photoshop.

2   Choose File > Open and then navigate to and open the file **Beach_sRGB.jpg** in the Color Management in Mac OS X Book Files > Lessons > Lesson05 folder on your hard drive.

Photoshop presents the Embedded Profile Mismatch dialog.

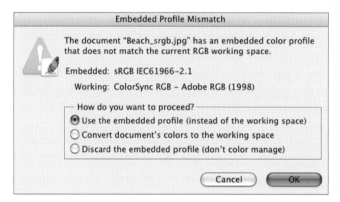

This warning appears because the camera that captured this image embedded an sRGB profile into the file, but Photoshop's RGB working space is set to Adobe RGB (1998). Photoshop offers the following choices for handling the conflict:

▶   "Use the embedded profile (instead of the working space)" — keeps the image in sRGB. When an image contains an embedded working-space profile, it is best to use this profile as the working space rather than convert it to a different working space. If you configured Photoshop's color Settings according to the exercise earlier in this lesson, this option will be selected by default.

▶   "Convert document's colors to the working space" — converts the image from the source space, in this case sRGB, to the selected working space, which is Adobe RGB (1998). There is no benefit to converting it to a different working space, unless the source space is a camera profile.

▶   "Discard the embedded profile" — ignores the embedded profile and opens the image in Photoshop in a generic RGB space. The image will be edited in the working space, but will not be tagged with a profile.

3 Make sure "Use the embedded profile (instead of the working space)" is checked, and then click OK.

Photoshop opens the image using the embedded profile as the working space.

4 Notice that Photoshop displays the sRGB working-space profile in the information area in the lower left of the image window. If the information area reads differently, choose Document Profile from the pop-up menu next to the area.

5 Quit Photoshop without saving your changes.

Importing Images with a Custom Camera Profile

If you have a custom profile for your camera—such as one you created in Lesson 4—you can use it as the source color space when you open an image in Photoshop. Here's how.

> **NOTE ▶** When using a custom profile, it is important to turn off the use of any working-space profile in your camera.

1 Launch Photoshop and open the sample file **Food.jpg**, located in the Color Management in Mac OS X Book Files > Lessons > Lesson05 folder of your hard drive.

2 Select Image > Mode > Assign Profile.

3 From the Profile pop-up menu, select D1X_2020.

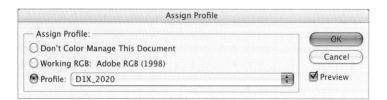

This instructs Photoshop to use the D1X_2020 camera profile as the source space for the image. The profile, similar to the profile built in Lesson 4 using ColorEyes 20/20, was created from an image taken by the same camera that photographed the **Food.jpg** image. Toggle the Preview option on and off to see the difference, which is most noticeable in the napkins and placemat.

The use of a custom camera profile results in more accurate colors. However, camera profiles do not make good editing spaces, as they often contain a much smaller gamut than working-space profiles and because they are device dependent. It's a good idea to convert the image to the working space before editing.

4   Select Image > Mode > Convert to Profile.

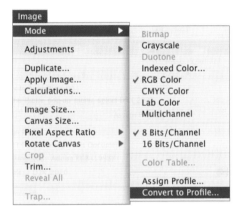

5   In the Convert to Profile dialog, select Adobe RGB (1998) as the Destination Space Profile.

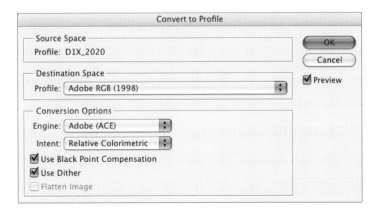

This will convert the image from the source space, the custom camera profile, to the destination space, the Adobe RGB (1998) working space.

6   Click OK to convert the image.

> **TIP** ▸ You can compare the gamut of your camera profile to a working-space profile using the ColorSync Utility.

Importing Images from Cameras Without Color-Management Support
If your digital camera does not support working-space and embedded profiles, and you don't have a custom camera profile, the best workflow option is to convert the captured image into Photoshop's working space. Photoshop won't change the file but will use the working space to interpret the data.

1   Launch Photoshop and open the file **Beach_untagged.jpg**, located in the Color Management in Mac OS X Book Files > Lessons > Lesson05 folder on your hard drive.

Because there is no profile embedded in the image file, Photoshop will present the Missing Profile dialog.

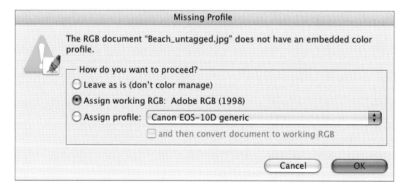

2   Select "Assign working RGB: Adobe RGB (1998)" and click OK.

Photoshop doesn't change the image data but does use the specified working-space profile to interpret the data. If the image is later edited in a different working space, Photoshop will use this assigned space, Adobe RGB (1998), to interpret the difference between the two working spaces. When you save the file, the working-space profile will be embedded.

Importing RAW Digital Camera Files

When a digital camera saves a JPEG or TIFF file, it performs a variety of processing tasks, such as tonal and color adjustments, sharpening, and compression. These modifications cannot be undone, and they can remove details from the image. For example, when a camera performs a color-space transformation on an image, color data may be permanently lost. As an alternative, many digital cameras support a file format—known as RAW—that contains unmodified data captured by the camera's sensor.

Each camera manufacturer has its own RAW file format and application to convert the files to more popular formats for use in design and imaging applications. The conversion is performed on the computer, where the photographer can adjust the image an unlimited number of times without the risk of permanently losing data. In addition to camera-manufacturer RAW converters, there are several third-party solutions, including the Adobe Camera Raw feature in Photoshop.

Working with RAW files in a color-managed workflow is slightly different from working with digital images in standard file formats. The workflow depends largely on the RAW conversion application. Let's try it first using Adobe Camera Raw, and then a third-party application, Phase One's C1 Pro RAW.

Image Processing with Adobe Camera Raw

Adobe has included RAW image conversion in Photoshop, in the form of Adobe Camera Raw (ACR). ACR supports a wide variety of RAW camera formats and provides powerful conversion options. Because ACR comes with Photoshop CS and supports a large number of RAW formats, many digital photographers choose ACR for their RAW workflow.

ACR takes advantage of Photoshop's color-management capabilities to provide a color-managed workflow for RAW file conversion.

> **TIP** If your camera's RAW format is not supported in Photoshop CS, check the Adobe Web site for a Camera Raw update.

1 Launch Photoshop and open the file **Junction.NEF**, located in the Color Management in Mac OS X Book Files > Lessons > Lesson05 folder on your hard drive. Photoshop detects that you are opening a RAW file and launches Adobe Camera Raw.

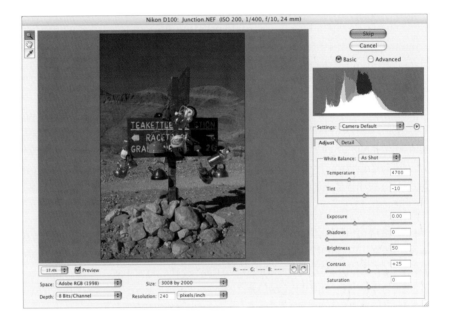

ACR uses generic source profiles for each camera: one for daylight and one for tungsten lighting. These profiles are embedded in ACR and can't be changed. You cannot select a different input profile for your camera, either. Adobe believes this approach will produce satisfactory results for most Photoshop users.

2 Choose Adobe RGB (1998) from the Space pop-up menu.

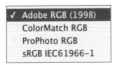

This sets the destination profile for the conversion process. Photoshop will convert from the source profile, which it automatically selects based on the type of RAW file, to the selected working-space profile. ACR limits the working-space profiles to four options. Adobe RGB (1998) provides the best-balanced working-space profile.

You typically won't see any changes between these choices in the ACR preview. This is because the gamut of most cameras is much smaller than any of the four supported working-space profiles.

3   Click OK. ACR opens the file in the selected working space.

The file is now in the selected working space, as noted in the information area in the lower left of the window.

4 Choose File > Save As.

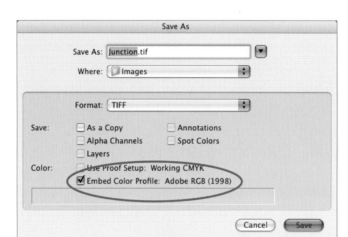

When you save the file, Photoshop will embed the working-space profile, as long as the selected file format supports embedded profiles.

NOTE ▶ Photoshop will alert you if you choose an image file format that does not support embedded profiles.

If you want to use custom camera profiles in your workflow, you will need to use RAW-conversion software that includes more advanced color-management capabilities.

5 Click Cancel to quit out of Adobe Camera Raw without changing the image.

RAW Image Processing with Capture One

If you want more control over the color-management portion of the RAW-conversion workflow, consider a third-party product. These products are not a replacement for Photoshop, but they do provide more control and automation for RAW conversion.

This exercise uses Phase One's C1 Pro RAW conversion application; a trial version of this software comes on this book's CD. If you have a different third-party RAW-conversion tool, look for comparable commands and functions in that application.

C1 Pro provides control over the conversion process, including both the source and destination color spaces. It also includes capabilities that support the batch conversion of images into multiple output files. For example, it can automatically convert a group of RAW files into CMYK TIFF files for press, RGB TIFF files for desktop photo printers, and RGB JPEG files for use on the Web—all with different file formats and destination color-space profiles.

NOTE ▶ If you haven't installed the trial version of Phase One's C1 Pro from this book's CD to your hard drive, do so now before continuing.

1   Copy the images **Carmel.CRW** and **Vail.CRW** from the Color Management in Mac OS X Book Files > Lessons > Lesson05 folder on your hard drive to Users > *User name* > Pictures > Capture One Default Session > Captures folder.

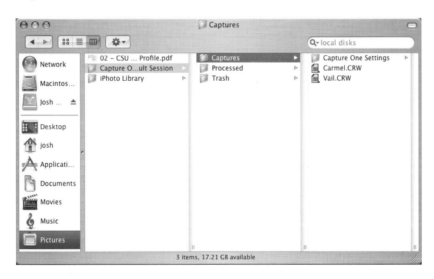

C1 Pro monitors this Captures folder for new RAW images, and then processes them according to the workflows set up by the user. The resulting files are placed in the Processed folder.

NOTE ▶ If you have your own RAW images that you'd like to use for this exercise, just copy them to the Captures folder. Be aware, however, that when this book went to press, C1 Pro for Mac OS X did not support the Nikon NEF RAW format.

2 Launch C1 Pro, located in the Applications folder on your hard drive, and choose C1 Pro > Preferences.

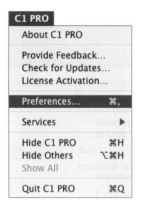

3 Click the Color Management icon.

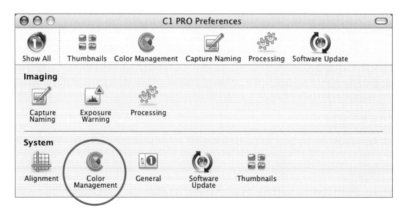

4   Click the Camera Profile button.

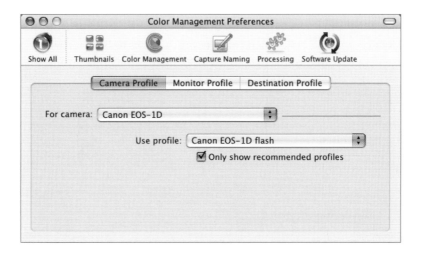

The Camera Profile Preferences pane lets you define which ICC profile C1 Pro will use as the source profile for each camera. The camera type is determined from data in the RAW file.

5   Choose your camera from the "For camera" pop-up menu (Canon EOS-D30 in our example).

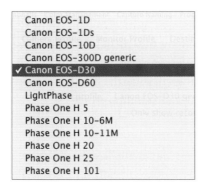

When you make this selection, "Canon EOS-D30 generic" automatically appears in the "Use profile" pop-up menu; it is the only available profile for the camera. To select any custom profiles, uncheck the "Only show recommended profiles" box, which restricts your choices to those provided by the manufacturer. In the case of the D30, there is only one profile.

6   Click the Monitor Profile button.

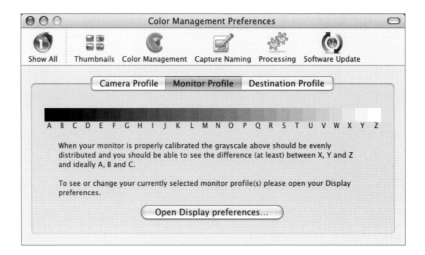

C1 Pro uses the default display profile setup in the ColorSync Preferences; you can click the "Open Display preferences" button to confirm or change it. The Monitor Profile Preferences window also includes a grayscale set of patches to help you determine if your display is properly calibrated. If the grayscale patches are not evenly distributed, you can click the "Open Display preferences" button to change your monitor profile.

7   Click the Destination Profile button.

C1 Pro uses the default rendering intent and quality settings in the profile. You can also choose custom settings specifically for C1 Pro. These settings will be used when converting RAW files into RGB, CMYK, and grayscale images.

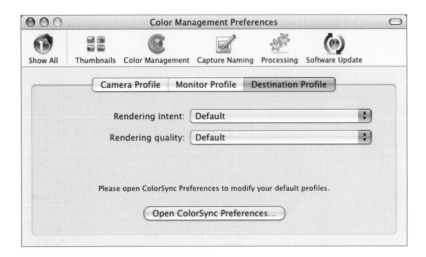

8   Click the red Close button to close C1 Pro's Preferences.

9   In the main C1 Pro window, click the Processing (gear) icon in the upper-left button bar.

The Processing section of C1 Pro is where each color-management workflow is defined. Workflows are listed in the Destinations panel in the upper-left area of the window. Each workflow can have a different destination profile for the images.

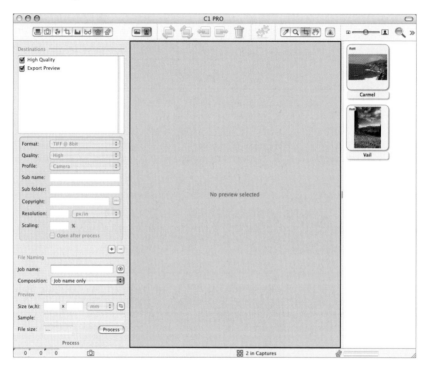

10 Click the Vail thumbnail image along the right side of the window to load it into the preview area.

At the bottom of the screen, C1 Pro displays the camera that was used to take the image, in this case a Canon EOS D30, and the profile it has assigned as the source profile for the image, in this case Canon EOS-D30 generic.

NOTE ▶ If you have selected a custom camera profile in the C1 Pro Preferences, it will be listed as the source profile.

11 In the Destinations area, click to select the High Quality workflow.

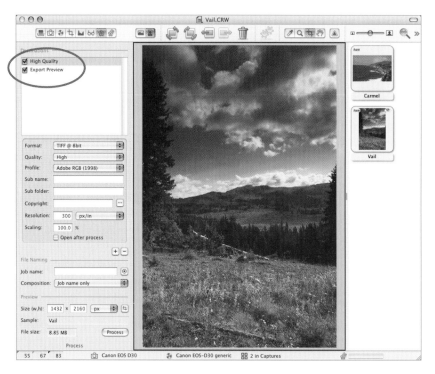

Selecting a Destination workflow enables you to specify format, quality, profile, resolution, and other options. These settings will be applied to all images output to the designated folder. Notice that the High Quality workflow by default uses Adobe RGB (1998) as the destination profile and 8-bit TIFF as the file format.

12 Click the + (plus sign) button on the left side of the window, just above the File Naming area, to create a new workflow.

13 Enter a name for your workflow. For example, I have set up a folder titled Peachpit.

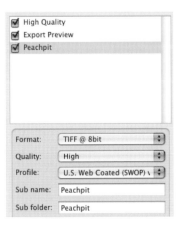

14 Click the Profile pop-up menu and choose a destination profile for your new workflow such as U.S. Web Coated (SWOP) v2.

C1 Pro will use the selected profile to convert the image. It will also embed the profile in the resulting file.

If you select Camera (at the top of the list), C1 Pro will convert the file to the selected file format and embed the camera profile (set in the Preferences) into the file. No color transformations will be applied.

15 Choose Image > Proof Profile, and choose the same profile that you selected in your new workflow.

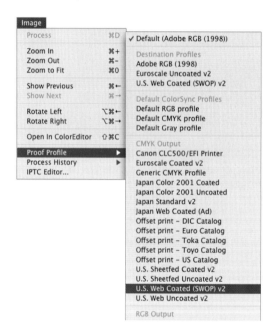

When a proof profile is selected, the display automatically adjusts to show a soft proof of the image, simulating what it will look when printed on the profiled device. C1 Pro indicates the source and destination profiles at the bottom of the screen.

16 When you have set up your workflow, click the Process button. C1 Pro will convert all images in the Captures folder into the appropriate file format and color space and save them in the Processed folder.

17 Quit C1 Pro.

Now when you open the processed image in Photoshop it will be converted to the selected file format—TIFF—and it will display in the Adobe RGB working space, which is the RGB working space we configured for Photoshop at the beginning of this lesson.

What You've Learned

- Photoshop's Color Settings controls how it displays, tags, and color manages images. Properly setting up Photoshop will ensure smoother and more predictable color output.

- When working with scanned images, color management can be applied in a stand-alone scanning application, in a Photoshop plug-in, or with Apple Image Capture.

- Color management of digital camera images in a standard file format such as JPEG or TIFF is easily performed in Photoshop by converting images from embedded or custom camera profiles to the Photoshop working-space profile.

- Digital camera RAW files require more processing but include more original (unprocessed) data. Applications such as Adobe Camera Raw and C1 Pro provide color-management conversion options.

6

Lesson Files   Color Management in Mac OS X Book Files > Lessons > Lesson06

Time   This lesson takes approximately 90 minutes to complete.

Goals   Set up soft-proofing to predict output from your printer

Perform a gamut check to see which colors are unprintable

Understand how Photoshop handles color printing

Embed profiles in images

Lesson 6

Image Proofing
and Output

The very first exercise in this book demonstrated the all-too-familiar frustrations of printing color images and artwork only to find out that the printed color looked quite different from how it appeared onscreen. Using color management while proofing images can dramatically increase the value of the proof by more accurately representing the image's final color. Now that we have created profiles for our devices and have properly configured Photoshop's Color Settings, we are ready to generate color-managed proofs with confidence.

Soft-Proofing Using Adobe Photoshop

Soft-proofing uses color management to simulate the output of your printer or press on your display. Accurate soft proofs can save time and money by reducing the number of interim hard-copy proofs (or comps) or press proofs that you need to generate.

Soft-proofing works on the assumption that the gamut of the display is generally larger than that of the printing device or process. For soft-proofing to work—for your prints to closely match what you see on your display—you'll need a calibrated display and high-quality profiles for your printer or printing process. Without those, it is difficult to get an accurate soft proof.

Adobe Photoshop includes a soft-proofing feature that provides advanced control over the onscreen simulation of colors. You can soft-proof an image for any device for which you have a profile, including printing presses.

NOTE ▶ Soft-proofing of artwork and page compositions is covered in Lessons 7 and 8.

1   Launch Adobe Photoshop by double-clicking its application name or icon in the Applications folder of your hard drive, or by clicking it in the Dock.

2   Choose File > Open, navigate to Color Management in Mac OS X Book Files > Lessons > Lesson06, and open the **Venice.tif** file.

NOTE ▶ If you have set Photoshop's RGB working space to a profile other than Adobe RGB (1998), the Photoshop Embedded Profile Mismatch dialog will appear when you open the files. Select the "Convert document's colors to the working space" option, and then click OK.

3 Choose View > Proof Setup and view the items in the submenu.

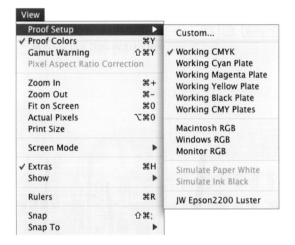

Photoshop offers a number of soft-proofing presets, including:

▶ Custom — lets you create a soft proof for your particular device.

▶ Working CMYK — simulates the output device selected as the CMYK working-space profile setting in the Color Settings dialog.

▶ Working Cyan, Magenta, Yellow, Black, CMY Plate(s) — previews one ink or all the inks used on press, based on the CMYK working-space profile. This is useful when preparing images for press.

▶ Macintosh RGB and Windows RGB — simulate what the image will look like on a Macintosh or Windows display, respectively. These are useful when preparing images for the Web and are only available when soft-proofing RGB images.

▶ Monitor RGB — displays the image using the current display profile and essentially reproduces the image the same way that an application that doesn't support color management would.

4   Choose the Custom proof setup. The Proof Setup dialog appears.

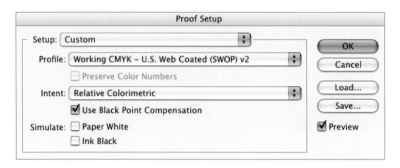

The Proof Setup dialog is where you choose the output device that you want to simulate onscreen and determine the settings for the soft proof. You can also save your settings as a preset.

5   Choose a printer profile from the Profile pop-up menu, such as JW E220 PremLstr 1_27_04.icc in my example.

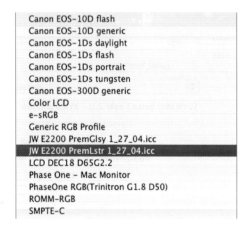

Photoshop displays a list of profiles for RGB, CMYK, and Grayscale devices, including working spaces, organized by profile class.

If you select a profile that is in the same color mode as the document's working space, the Preserve Color Numbers option becomes available. The **Venice.tif** image is an RGB image, as is the profile for my Epson Stylus Photo 2200; therefore the option becomes available.

6   If Preserve Color Numbers is available, deselect it.

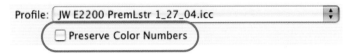

Deselecting Preserve Color Numbers will perform an accurate soft proof to the selected device.

7   Choose Intent > Relative Colorimetric.

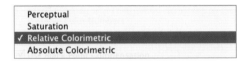

The rendering intent determines how colors that are out of gamut for the selected device are mapped to in-gamut colors. Relative Colorimetric, which is suitable for photographic images, compares the highlight of the source color space to that of the destination color space and shifts out-of-gamut colors to the closest reproducible color in the destination color space. It preserves more of the original colors in an image than the Perceptual intent.

8   Make sure Use Black Point Compensation is checked. This instructs Photoshop to adjust the display simulation to give a better preview for the actual black on output.

TIP   Check the Preview box to immediately see the effect of a selection on the open image.

9   If it's available, check Simulate Paper White. When Simulate Paper White is selected, Simulate Ink Black is automatically selected and grayed out.

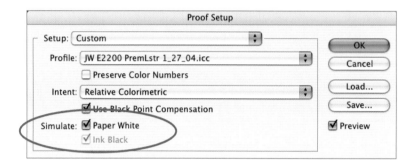

Simulate Paper White allows you to add the color of the paper to the proof. This is often an off-white or yellowish color. (Photoshop accomplishes this preview by modifying the rendering intent.) Similarly, Simulate Ink Black uses the actual black, which may be a dark gray, in the simulation. These options, which are not supported by all profiles, improve the accuracy of your soft proof.

10 Click Save to save your settings as a preset. In the Save dialog that appears, give your proof setup an intuitive name. Photoshop automatically saves color settings in Macintosh HD > Users > *User name* > Library > Application Support > Adobe > Color > Proofing folder. Then click Save.

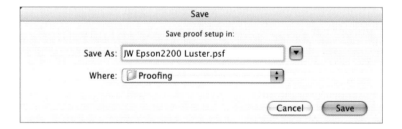

11 Choose View > Proof Setup and choose your new custom preset from the submenu.

Photoshop now displays the image as it will appear on the selected output device.

The name of the image in the title bar is appended with the Proof Setup name saved in the soft proof.

It's a good idea to create presets for different paper-and-ink combinations or for different printers so that you can soft-proof for all your color devices. After creating and saving custom presets, you can easily switch between them.

12 Select View > Proof Colors (or press Command-Y) to toggle the soft proof off and on.

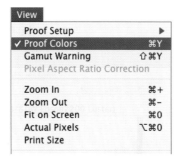

Certain profiles will have more dramatic results when they're viewed as soft proofs in Photoshop. For example, with a press profile such as U.S. Web Coated (SWOP) v2, used in the printing of this book, the image will look less vibrant and contrasty. It's also important to remember that the quality of the soft proof correlates directly to the quality of your display and device profiles. Finally, in order to get an accurate hard-copy proof, you'll need to know how to configure your print options. We'll learn about that as soon as we perform a gamut check.

Performing a Gamut Check

If you are soft-proofing an image that contains colors that cannot be reproduced by your printer, the soft proof on your screen is displayed with *gamut mapping*, as we learned in Lesson 1. Gamut mapping brings out-of-gamut colors into gamut. The rendering intent determines which in-gamut color is selected to replace the out-of-gamut color. If the colors are only slightly out of gamut, the effect may be subtle. In any case, it's often useful—even important—to know which colors are out of gamut.

NOTE ▶ For more on rendering intents, see Lesson 1.

Luckily, Photoshop offers a feature called the Gamut Warning, which allows you to see if any of the colors in an image will be out of gamut for your selected printing device. Gamut Warning uses the settings in Proof Setup to determine the target output device, and then it compares the colors in the image to the gamut of the profiled device. It displays any out-of-gamut colors in gray. The Gamut Warning is a useful feature in conjunction with soft-proofing.

1   Make sure that the **Venice.tif** image is still open in Photoshop and that your Custom proof setup from the previous exercise is chosen.

2   Choose View > Gamut Warning.

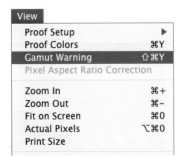

Photoshop displays the image with the out-of-gamut colors in gray.

The areas shaded in gray (in the flowers at the bottom of the image) are colors that cannot be reproduced by the output device denoted by the selected profile in the Proof Setup dialog.

3   Toggle the Gamut Warning on and off by pressing Shift-Command-Y to see the affected colors.

> **TIP** You can perform additional color corrections with Gamut Warning on to further optimize your image based on the gamut limitations of the selected device.

Printing Color-Managed Images

Photoshop offers powerful color-management control when printing— if you know how to set it up properly. Printing from Photoshop provides several advantages:

- You can easily send one image to multiple devices, and even generate separations for press output, with as close a match as possible between the devices.

- Photoshop supports both RGB and CMYK workflows.

- An image printed from Photoshop will match the onscreen soft proof or device proof as closely as possible.

The key to successfully printing with color management is to ensure that color management is applied only once. This means disabling any color-management features in the printer driver and operating system to ensure that Photoshop is the only place that color management is being applied.

1   In Photoshop, make sure that the **Venice.tif** image is still open.

2   Choose File > Page Setup.

3   Select your printer from the "Format for" pop-up menu.

4   Confirm that Paper Size is set to US Letter (or A4 if you're outside the US), that the Orientation is set to landscape, and that Scale is 100%, as shown in the following image.

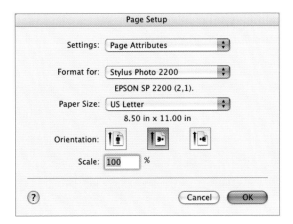

5   Click OK.

6   Choose File > Print with Preview.

7   In the Print dialog that appears, check the Show More Options box and select Color Management from the pop-up menu just below it.

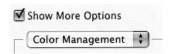

8   Under Source Space, confirm that Document: Adobe RGB (1998) is selected. This tells Photoshop to use the working space as the source space.

NOTE ▶ The Source Space Proof option is used to perform device simulation on the output device. So, for example, if you select SWOP as your source space proof setting, you can then simulate SWOP on the device you select for your print space. To configure the source space proof properly, first select the device you want to simulate in the Proof Setup as covered in the previous exercise. This feature will be covered in more detail in Lesson 9.

9   Under Print Space, choose the profile for your printer from the Profile pop-up menu. This tells Photoshop to color manage the file from the working space to the printer-profile space.

10   Select Relative Colorimetric from the Intent pop-up menu. Make sure the Use Black Point Compensation option is selected.

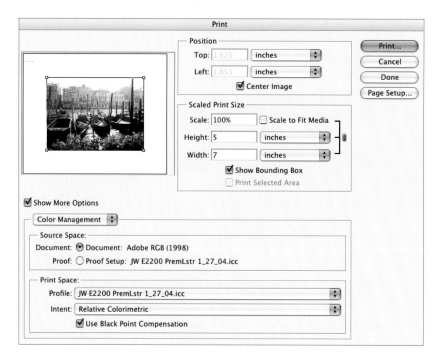

NOTE ▶ Color is subjective. If you find that the Relative Colorimetric intent does not produce a good screen-to-print match for your particular image or images, choose a different rendering intent, such as Perceptual.

11   Click Print.

12 In the Print driver dialog that appears, choose your printer from the Printer pop-up menu.

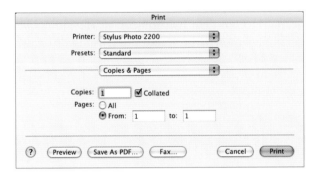

13 Click the Copies & Pages pop-up menu to locate your printer's media settings, and then choose the correct paper for your device. The location of the media option varies with each printer; look for it under a heading such as Print Settings. The following image shows the Epson Print Settings menu, with Premium Luster Photo Paper chosen from the Media Type pop-up menu. In addition, disable any automatic settings. For example, I chose Advanced Settings, also shown in the following figure, instead of Automatic.

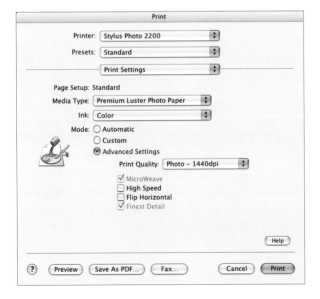

14 Click the Copies & Pages pop-up menu again, locate your printer's color-management options, and *turn them off*. The location of these options varies with each printer; look for them under a heading such as Custom, Advanced, or Color Management. The following image shows the Color Management option in the Epson Stylus Photo 2200 printer driver, with No Color Adjustment selected.

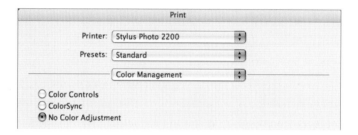

15 Click Print to start printing.

TIP Save these settings to use again when printing with the profile by choosing Save As from the Presets pop-up menu. It's important to always print with the same settings—changing the resolution or paper type will affect the results.

Comparing Soft and Hard Proofs

Now is the moment you've been waiting for: You've got the soft proof of the image onscreen, and you've printed it using Photoshop's color-management features (and no other color management), and you're ready to compare the results. Keep in mind that even if you have done everything right, the print may not match the screen *exactly*. It's extremely difficult to obtain a perfect match. The goal is to get a close match to gain predictability so that you can make adjustments, corrections, and separations with confidence. No proofing system will match colors exactly; the trick is to learn to interpret the differences, and this is accomplished through experience.

Optimizing Viewing Conditions

There are two schools of wisdom when it comes to viewing conditions. The first says that you should view your printed output in a controlled lighting environment that is consistent with the computer environment in which you display the images. In other words, if your display is calibrated to D65, you should view the printed images in a 6500-kelvin light booth. Controlled lighting sources range from relatively low-cost light bulbs that fit into standard lamps to very expensive light booths, like the kind you'll find next to a printing press. The more expensive solutions typically output two or more common color temperatures, such as 5000 K and 6500 K.

The second school of wisdom—to which I subscribe—is that your prints may be viewed under any number of lighting conditions—at home, in outdoor daylight, in a studio, in an office, or even on an airplane, for example. Given that you cannot control the conditions in which your final color will be viewed, it does not make sense to invest in expensive color-controlled viewing environments when you evaluate proofs. Instead, rely on limited, reasonable controls. For example, you can:

- Avoid extreme lighting conditions, such as direct sunlight. Opt instead for daylight filtered through a window.

- Use a flat, neutral-color paint around your computer workstation.

- Wear neutral-colored clothing when you view proofs.

- Use a hood on your display. Avoid direct light on the display.

I have found that a high-quality calibrated display, accurate profiles, and the right settings produce a very good match between my display and prints.

Assigning Profiles to Images

When profiles are embedded in images, there is little doubt as to the source of the data. Unfortunately, not all applications and devices embed profiles automatically.

When you save an image, Photoshop will automatically embed the working-space profile in the file. You can also tag an image with a profile other than the working space-profile so that it is embedded in the saved file.

NOTE ▶ Embedded profiles are supported in the Photoshop PSD, EPS, and PDF file formats as well as in TIFF, JPEG, and PICT files.

The Assign Profile function can be used to change the embedded profile in an image, or to assign a profile to an untagged image. Assigning a profile does not actually perform conversions; rather, changing the embedded profile tells Photoshop to interpret the data differently, which can change the image's appearance. You would typically use the Assign Profile command to assign a profile to an untagged image, and then use the Preview feature to view the results.

1   Launch Adobe Photoshop by double-clicking its application name or icon in the Applications folder of your hard drive or by clicking it in the Dock.

2   Choose File > Open, navigate to Color Management in Mac OS X Book Files > Lessons > Lesson06, and open the **Carmel_untagged.tif** file. The Missing Profile dialog appears.

The Missing Profile dialog that appears when you open an untagged image has the same functionality as the Assign Profile dialog, except the Assign Profile dialog can preview the results. For the purpose of this exercise, we'll open the image without assigning a profile.

3 Make sure "Leave as is (don't color manage)" is selected, and then click OK.

When Photoshop opens the image, notice that the information box in the lower-left corner of the window says Untagged RGB.

4 Choose Image > Mode > Assign Profile.

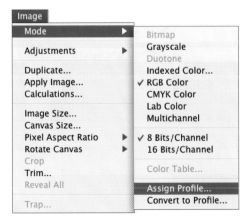

The Assign Profile dialog appears.

Assign Profile

Assign Profile:
○ Don't Color Manage This Document
◉ Working RGB: Adobe RGB (1998)
○ Profile: Wide Gamut RGB

OK
Cancel
☑ Preview

The Assign Profile function has three options for changing the embedded profile.

The first option, Don't Color Manage This Document, removes the embedded profile from an image. When you choose this option, Photoshop will use the working-space profile as the source of the data. This is useful if you are sending the image to someone who has requested that the image *not* have an embedded profile.

The second option, Working RGB, will tag the image with the working space assigned in the Color Settings dialog. In our example, that is Adobe RGB (1998). This option is useful if an image is untagged or is tagged incorrectly, and you want to work with it in the default working space.

The third option, the Profile pop-up menu, allows you to assign any profile of the same color mode to the image. This is useful for assigning input profiles to digital images and scans, especially as you can see the results of the selection. Once you assign the profile, you will want to use Convert to Profile (described in later steps) to convert it to the working space.

5 Choose the Canon EOS-D30 generic profile from the Profile pop-up menu.

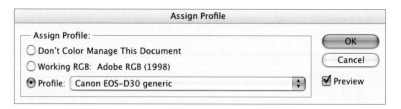

Assign Profile

Assign Profile:
○ Don't Color Manage This Document
○ Working RGB: Adobe RGB (1998)
◉ Profile: Canon EOS-D30 generic

OK
Cancel
☑ Preview

TIP ▶ Toggle the Preview box on and off to see the difference.

6 Click OK.

Photoshop displays the image onscreen using the camera profile as the source. The information box in the lower-left corner of the image window now indicates that Photoshop is using the embedded generic Canon EOS profile as the working space.

Using input profiles as working spaces is not ideal, in part because camera and scanner profiles are device dependent. The Convert to Profile command can be used to convert the image to a desirable working-space profile.

7 Choose Image > Mode > Convert to Profile.

The Convert to Profile dialog appears.

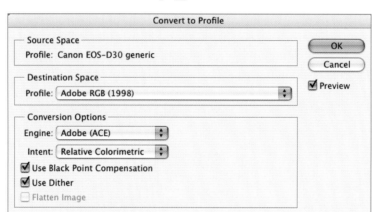

Convert to Profile enables you to convert an image from the embedded document profile space, listed under Source Space, to another profile space. If the image is opened without a profile, Photoshop will use the working space as the source space.

This feature is useful for converting images from one color space to another, such as when you are separating images for press.

Compared with making a color-mode change, using Convert to Profile provides greater control over the conversion process, including the ability to more easily change the destination space and the conversion options. Photoshop's mode-change commands (choosing Image > Mode > CMYK or Image > Mode > RGB, for example) use the preferences in Color Settings; if you want to change the destination space, you have to change your preferences.

The Engine, Intent, Use Black Point Compensation, and Use Dither conversion options are the same as those in the Color Settings dialog, which were described in detail in Lesson 5. The Flatten Image setting is used to flatten the layers of an image upon conversion, and it is only active when the image has multiple layers.

8 Choose U.S. Web Uncoated v2 from the Destination Space Profile pop-up menu.

9   Toggle the Preview option off and on to see the (subtle) changes.

10 Choose Adobe RGB (1998) from the Destination Space Profile pop-up menu and then click OK.

We are keeping the image in the Adobe RGB (1998) working space, converted from the Canon EOS-D30 source profile.

11 Choose File > Save As.

The Save As dialog appears.

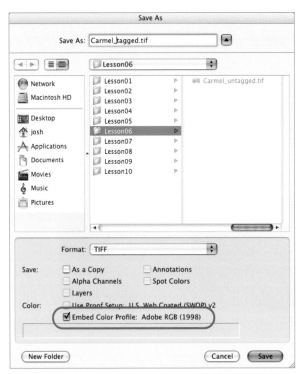

Photoshop's Save and Save As dialogs both allow you to embed the working-space profile. This option is checked by default.

12 Change the filename to Carmel_tagged.tif, and click Save.

This file was brought into Photoshop, untagged, from a Canon EOS D30 digital camera. Using the Assign Profile and Convert to Profile functions, we assigned the camera profile to the image, converted it to the working-space profile, and saved it with the Adobe RGB (1998) working-space profile embedded in the image file.

13 Quit Photoshop.

The Assign Profile and Convert to Profile functions operate much like the Missing Profile and Profile Mismatch dialogs, but provide more control and flexibility over the process.

What You've Learned

- Soft-proofing can save time and money by reducing the number of prints necessary to get the desired results.

- Performing a gamut check allows you to see what colors are out of gamut for your printing device, which can reduce unwanted surprises and costly reprints.

- The key to accurate color-managed printing from Photoshop is making sure that color-management is applied only once—by Photoshop, not by the operating system or printer driver.

- Photoshop's Assign Profile command can be used to change the embedded profile in an image or to assign a profile to an untagged image.

7

Lesson Files	Color Management in Mac OS X Book Files > Lessons > Lesson07
Time	This lesson takes approximately 2 hours to complete.
Goals	Set up color management in Adobe Creative Suite applications using the Adobe Common Color Architecture
	Color manage both new and existing artwork files
	Soft-proof an illustration to simulate an output device
	Embed profiles in artwork and save in the Adobe Portable Document Format
	Print illustrations with color management

Using the Adobe Common Color Architecture

The Adobe Creative Suite applications, including Photoshop, Illustrator, Acrobat, InDesign and GoLive, all share a color-management implementation known as the Adobe Common Color Architecture. This ensures that all of the Creative Suite applications support color management in the same way.

We learned how to set up and use most of the features of this architecture in Photoshop as part of Lesson 5. In this lesson, we'll learn how use the Color Settings in other Creative Suite applications, how to apply these features in Adobe Illustrator to color manage vector artwork, and how to generate color-managed Adobe PDF files.

Sharing Adobe Color Settings

One of the benefits of the Adobe Common Color Architecture is the shared Color Settings file. This enables you to set the preferences once and use them throughout the Adobe Creative Suite. By using the same settings throughout the suite, you ensure that all of the applications handle color the same way.

NOTE ▶ All of the Adobe Creative Suite applications are available as 30-day trial versions on the Adobe Web site.

Configuring Illustrator Color Settings

Let's begin by setting up the Color Settings for Illustrator, much as we did for Photoshop.

TIP ▶ Set up Photoshop first, as it has more options than the other applications in the suite.

1   Launch Adobe Illustrator CS, which should be located in the Applications folder on your hard drive.

2   Choose Edit > Color Settings.

The Color Settings dialog appears.

The default setting is Emulate Adobe Illustrator 6.0, which is essentially the same as turning color management off.

3   Click the Settings pop-up menu and choose the custom Color Settings file that you created (and saved) in Photoshop in Lesson 5.

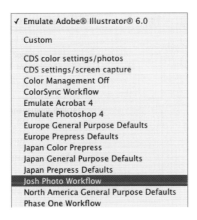

The settings, including those for Working Spaces and Color Management Policies, now match the ones we're using in Photoshop.

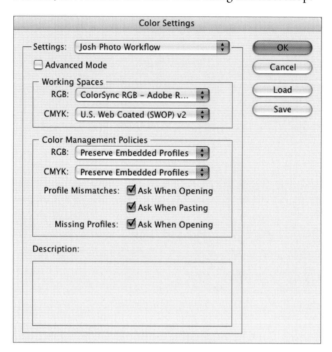

4   Check the Advanced Mode box if it isn't already checked.

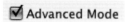

You can now see that even the advanced options, such as the chosen color engine and use of black point compensation, are also consistent with the ones we're using in Photoshop.

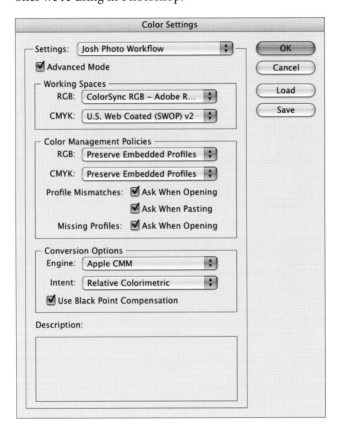

5   Click OK to close Illustrator's Color Settings.

If you didn't save your custom Color Settings in Photoshop, you can go back and do that now, and then choose them in Illustrator. Alternatively, if you chose one of the presets in Photoshop, such as ColorSync Workflow or U.S. Prepress Defaults, choose that same preset in Illustrator. By using the same Color Settings in both applications, you ensure that the colors in files that are opened in both applications will be consistent both onscreen and when you print.

Configuring InDesign Color Settings

Images edited or manipulated in Adobe Photoshop, and artwork created in Adobe Illustrator, are often then incorporated into page layouts. Here's how to configure InDesign's Color Settings so that they're consistent with those in Photoshop and Illustrator.

NOTE ▶ Lesson 8 will cover color management in QuarkXPress.

1 Launch Adobe InDesign CS, which should be located in the Applications folder on your hard drive.

2 Choose Edit > Color Settings.

The Color Settings dialog appears.

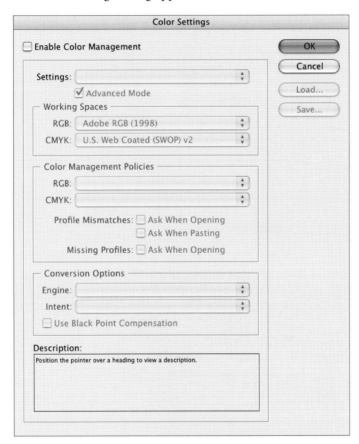

3   Check the Enable Color Management box.

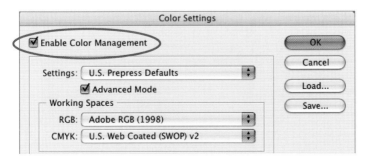

NOTE ▶ Advanced Mode is on by default. If the Advanced Mode box isn't checked, check it now.

4   Click the Settings pop-up menu and choose the custom Color Settings file that you created (and saved) in Photoshop in Lesson 5.

InDesign's Color Settings, including those for Working Spaces, Color Management Policies, and Conversion Options, now match the ones we're using in Photoshop and Illustrator.

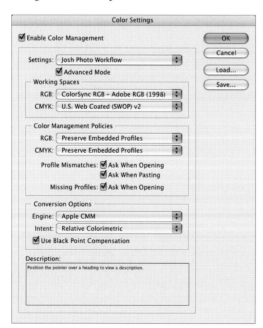

5   Click OK to close InDesign's Color Settings.

6   Press Command-Q to quit InDesign.

Again, if you didn't save your custom Color Settings in Photoshop, you can go back and do that now, and then choose them in InDesign. Alternatively, if you chose one of the presets in Photoshop, such as ColorSync Workflow or U.S. Prepress Defaults, choose that same preset in InDesign. By using the same Color Settings in both applications, as well as in Illustrator if you use Illustrator, you ensure that the colors in files that are opened in all applications will be consistent both onscreen and when you print.

Configuring Acrobat Color Settings

Adobe Acrobat can be used to facilitate the review and approval of designs and documents, to soft-proof, and to generate final output. It allows you to create and view Adobe PDF, or Portable Document Format, files. Adobe PDF files can be opened and shared across all of Adobe's professional design applications. That's why it's important to have the Color Settings in Adobe Acrobat match those of Photoshop, Illustrator, and InDesign.

1   Launch Adobe Acrobat 6.0 Professional, which should be located in the Applications folder on your hard drive.

2   Choose Acrobat > Preferences.

3   In the Preferences dialog that appears, choose Color Management from the list pane on the left.

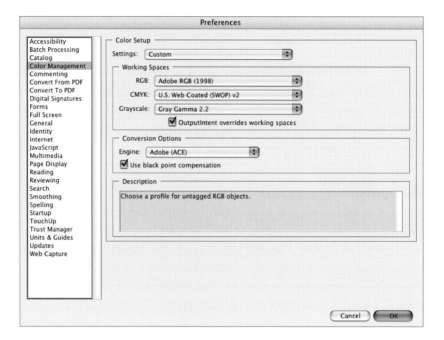

Acrobat's Color Management Preferences contain similar settings to those of other Adobe Creative Suite applications, except that the Acrobat preferences are used only for *displaying* color data.

4   Click the Settings pop-up menu and choose the custom Color Settings file that you created (and saved) in Photoshop in Lesson 5.

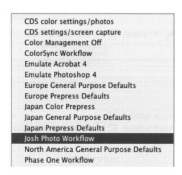

The settings, including those for Working Spaces and Conversion Options, now match the ones we're using in Photoshop, Illustrator, and InDesign.

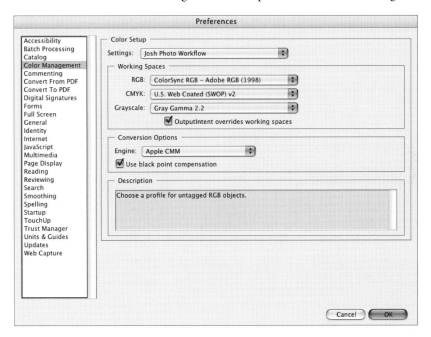

Notice that Acrobat contains a new option, a check box called "OutputIntent overrides working spaces."

![OutputIntent overrides working spaces]

5   Make sure "OutputIntent overrides working spaces" is checked. This instructs Acrobat that if the Adobe PDF document includes an output-intent profile, it should be used instead of the document working space for viewing and printing.

6   Click OK to close Acrobat's Preferences dialog.

7   Press Command-Q to quit Acrobat.

Once again, if you didn't save your custom Color Settings in Photoshop, you can go back and do that now, and then choose them in Acrobat. And if you chose one of the other presets in Photoshop, such as ColorSync Workflow or U.S. Prepress Defaults, you should choose that same preset in Acrobat (and Illustrator and InDesign). By using the same Color Settings in all applications, you ensure that the colors in files that are opened in all of them will be consistent both onscreen and when you print.

Color Managing Artwork

Now that we have configured Illustrator's Color Settings, we can create, edit, and output artwork in a color-managed environment. The color workflow in Illustrator uses the same concepts and features as in Photoshop, with a few exceptions.

Creating New Color-Managed Artwork

When you create a new document in Illustrator, you choose either RGB or CMYK for the color mode, which in turn defines the color management that's applied to the file.

1   Launch Illustrator if it is not still open on your Mac.

2   Choose File > New.

     The New Document dialog appears.

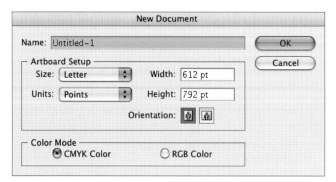

3   Notice the CMYK Color and RGB Color radio buttons.

When you choose CMYK Color for your new document's Color Mode, Illustrator uses the CMYK working space you've defined in Color Settings for that CMYK document. When you choose RGB, Illustrator uses the RGB working space you've defined for the new RGB document.

4   Click Cancel.

Defining the working space of new documents is easy enough, but what happens if you're working in one color space, such as CMYK, but accidentally (or even intentionally) define a color from a different color space, such as RGB, while you're editing? When you select a color from a color space that is different from the document color space, Illustrator will use the default profiles (as defined in Color Settings) to convert the color to the working space. For example, if you define an RGB color in a CMYK document, Illustrator will automatically convert the RGB values to CMYK, using the RGB working-space profile as the source, and the CMYK working-space profile as the destination. Keeping everything in the document working space ensures accuracy and portability.

Working with Preexisting Artwork

When you open an Illustrator or EPS file, Illustrator applies its Color Settings' Color Management Policies to the file. If the file is already tagged and its working-space profile is the same as the one you've selected in Illustrator, there's no problem. Sometimes, however, you'll encounter one of two situations: the files will be untagged (not color managed), or they'll be color managed, but there's a conflict, and you may or may not know the source data and profiles used. Let's explore how to handle these two situations.

Opening Untagged Artwork

1   Launch Adobe Illustrator CS if it isn't already open on your Mac.

2   Choose File > Open and the file **Yellowstone Map.ai**, which comes with Adobe Illustrator CS and is located in the Macintosh HD > Applications > Adobe Illustrator CS > Sample Files > Sample Art folder.

Illustrator presents the Missing Profile dialog.

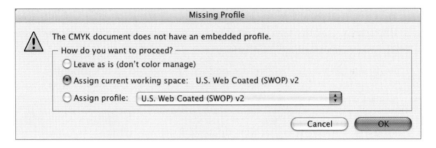

As in Photoshop, Illustrator presents you with three choices for handling the data:

▶ "Leave as is (don't color manage)" — uses the working-space profile (CMYK in this case) as the source of the data but does not tag the file.

▶ "Assign current working space" — uses the working-space profile (a CMYK SWOP profile in this case) as the source of the data and tags the file with the profile. This is generally the best option if you do not know the source of the data.

▶ "Assign profile" — allows you to select a profile for the document. If you know the source of the data, you should select the appropriate profile.

NOTE ▶ If you choose "Assign profile" and then select a different profile for the working space, Illustrator will present you with the Assigned Profile Mismatch dialog, asking you if you want to convert to the working space, or leave the current document space. You should select the embedded profile.

3   Since we don't know the source of this data, select "Assign current working space" and then click OK to open the file.

Once the file is open, Illustrator color manages the document using the current working space.

4   Press Command-W to close **Yellowstone Map.ai**.

Opening Artwork with Embedded Profiles

1   Choose File > Open, navigate to the file **Logo.eps** in the Color Management
in Mac OS X Book Files > Lessons > Lesson07 folder on your hard drive,
and then click OK.

This file has an embedded profile that is different from the working-space
profile we have defined for Illustrator, so Illustrator presents the Embedded
Profile Mismatch dialog.

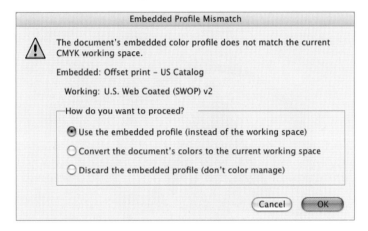

As with Photoshop, the Embedded Profile Mismatch dialog offers three
choices for handling the data:

▶   "Use the embedded profile (instead of the working space)" — uses the
embedded profile as the working space. When artwork contains an embedded working-space profile, it is best to use this profile as the working space,
rather than convert it to a different working space. If you configured
Illustrator's Color Settings according to the exercise earlier in this lesson,
this option will be selected by default, and in general it is the best option.

▶   "Convert the document's colors to the current working space" —
converts the image from the source space, in this case Offset print – US
Catalog, to the selected working space, which is U.S. Web Coated (SWOP) v2.
There is no benefit to converting it to a different working space. When the
file is printed, separated for press, or converted to a Web graphic, it will be
converted to the appropriate destination profile.

▶ "Discard the embedded profile (don't color manage)" — ignores the embedded profile and opens the image in Illustrator, using the working-space profile to interpret the color values. The file will not be tagged with a profile.

2   Make sure "Use the embedded profile (instead of the working space)" is selected and then click OK to open the file.

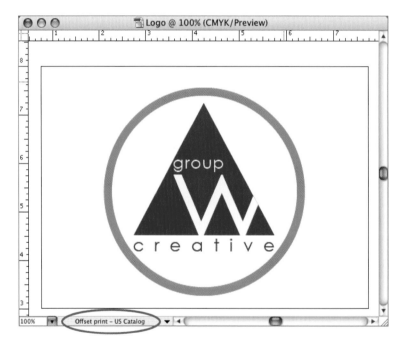

Once the file is open, Illustrator color manages the document using the embedded profile, as illustrated in the information area in the lower left of the document window.

3   Press Command-W to close **Logo.eps**.

Working with Placed Files in Illustrator

Color management of vector artwork gets more complicated when you place artwork or images in Illustrator from another application. When you place an image into an Illustrator document, it includes a linked copy of the image in the file. How Illustrator color manages the placed art depends on the color state of the file:

- If the placed file does not contain an embedded profile and is in the same color mode as the Illustrator document, no color conversion is performed on the placed file.

- If the placed file does not contain an embedded profile and is in a different color mode from the Illustrator document, the file is converted using the working-space profile as the source. For example, if you place an RGB image into a CMYK illustration, the default RGB working-space profile is used as the source and the default CMYK working-space profile is used as the destination.

- If the placed file contains an embedded profile but is in a different color mode from the Illustrator document, the color values are converted using the embedded profile as the source and the document's working space as the destination.

- If the placed file contains an embedded profile and is in the same color mode as the Illustrator document, the conversion is dictated by the Color Management Policies set in Illustrator's Color Settings, which we have configured to ask us when there is a mismatch or missing profile. In this case, Illustrator will ask if we want to perform the conversion according to the policy settings.

The best solution to simplify the process of compositing artwork with different source profiles is to first convert each file to the same working space upon opening the file, and then place or paste them into an Illustrator file.

Assigning Profiles to Untagged Artwork

If you have a file without an embedded profile, you can assign a profile to it in Illustrator either when opening the file (by choosing "Assign profile" in the Missing Profile dialog) or by using the Assign Profile command after the image is open. Here's how:

1 Launch Illustrator if it's not already open on your Mac, choose File > Open, and then navigate to and open **Yellowstone Map.ai**, located in the Macintosh HD > Applications > Adobe Illustrator CS > Sample Files > Sample Art folder.

Illustrator presents the Missing Profile dialog.

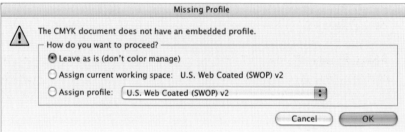

2 Select "Leave as is (don't color manage)," which instructs Illustrator not to assign a profile to the file, and then click OK.

3 In the information area at the bottom of the document window, choose Document Color Profile.

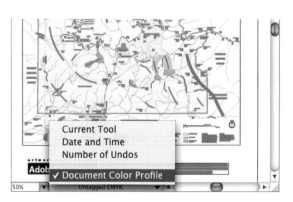

The information area should read "Untagged CMYK," indicating that the file has no embedded profile.

4   Choose Edit > Assign Profile.

The Assign Profile dialog appears.

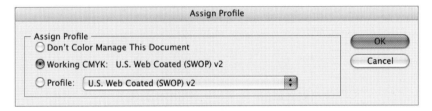

Assign Profile functions much like the Missing Profile dialog that is presented when you open a file that doesn't have a profile. Assign Profile lets you choose either the current working-space profile or a different profile for the file.

NOTE ▶ The "Don't Color Manage This Document" option removes a profile embedded in an image. Do not select it if you're trying to assign a profile to an untagged file.

5   Select Working CMYK and click OK. The file is now tagged with the working-space profile, as reflected in the information area at the bottom of the document window.

6   Choose File > Save as.

7 In the Save As dialog that appears, change the filename so that you don't overwrite the original, choose Adobe Illustrator Document from the Format pop-up menu, and click Save.

The Illustrator Options dialog appears with the Embed ICC Profiles option checked by default.

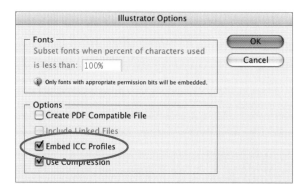

The Embed ICC Profiles option instructs Illustrator to embed the current working-space profile in the file. Illustrator supports embedding profiles in the Adobe Illustrator and Adobe PDF file formats. If you embed a profile in an EPS file, Illustrator converts it to a PostScript Color Space Array, the PostScript equivalent of a source profile. The only way to embed an ICC profile in an EPS file is to use Photoshop to convert it to a bitmap image and embed the profile when saving.

Alternatively, you can embed profiles in a bitmap file format such as TIFF via Illustrator's Export command. Illustrator also lets you embed profiles in JPEG files via the Save for Web command.

8   Make sure that Embed ICC Profiles is checked, and click OK to save the file.

Soft-Proofing in Illustrator

You can soft-proof artwork in Illustrator to simulate onscreen what it will look like when printed.

1   Open the file **Yellowstone Map.ai** file as described in the previous exercise.

2   Choose View > Proof Setup > Custom.

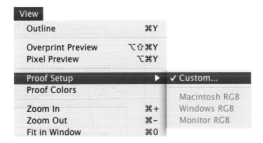

The Proof Setup dialog appears.

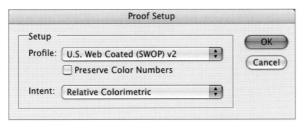

Much like the Photoshop Proof Setup, Illustrator lets you select the profile and rendering intent for the device you want to soft-proof.

3   Choose the profile of the device you wish to simulate from the Profile pop-up menu. I selected the custom profile for my Epson Stylus Photo 2200.

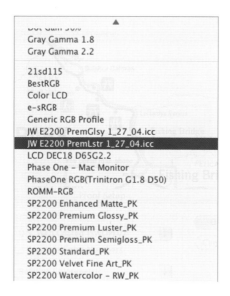

4   If it's available, make sure "Preserve color numbers" is unchecked.

"Preserve color numbers" instructs Illustrator to display the image as if it were printed to the device *without* using a profile. This option, which is available only for profiles in the same color space as the document, can help determine if the image needs to be converted using a profile, or if it can be sent straight to the device.

5   Choose Absolute Colorimetric from the Intent pop-up menu.

6   Click OK.

7   Choose View > Proof Colors to toggle on the soft proof.

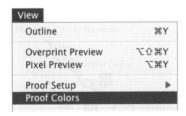

Yellowstone Map.ai is a large, complex illustration and may take a few seconds to redraw.

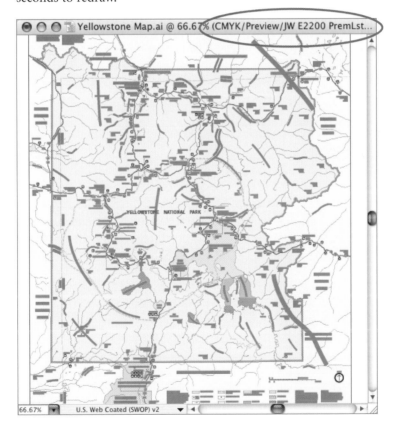

The name of the image in the title bar is appended with the name of the profile used in the soft proof.

8   Toggle the soft proof off and on by choosing View > Proof Colors a few
times, and compare the results. For this particular artwork and these profiles, the effects will be very subtle.

Printing Color-Managed Artwork

This exercise continues to use the Yellowstone map illustration to demonstrate
how to print a color-managed proof from Adobe Illustrator.

1   With **Yellowstone Map.ai** still open in Illustrator, choose File > Print.

The Illustrator Print dialog appears.

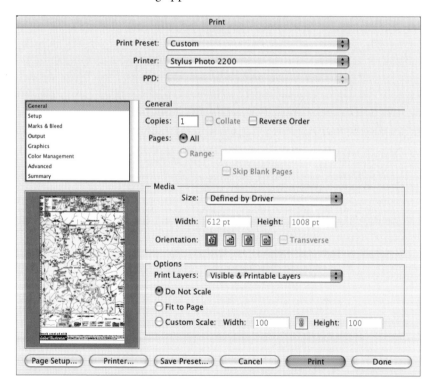

2   Make sure your color printer is chosen in the Printer pop-up menu.

3   Choose Color Management from the list pane on the left.

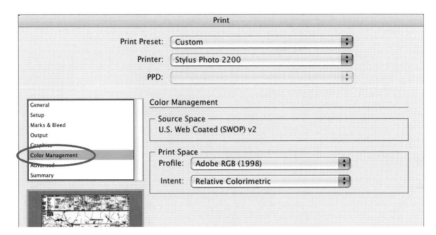

The Color Management section of the Print dialog displays the document's Source and Print Spaces.

4   In the Print Space area, choose the profile for your particular output device from the Profile pop-up menu. I chose my custom printer profile created by Chromix in Lesson 3, JW E2200 PremLstr 1_27_04.icc.

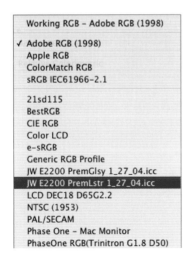

5   Choose a rendering intent from the Intent pop-up menu, such as Absolute Colorimetric.

Now Illustrator is ready to color manage the file when printed. However, as we explored in Photoshop in previous lessons, we must ensure that the printer driver does not apply additional color management, which could yield undesirable results.

6   Click the Printer button at the bottom of the dialog.

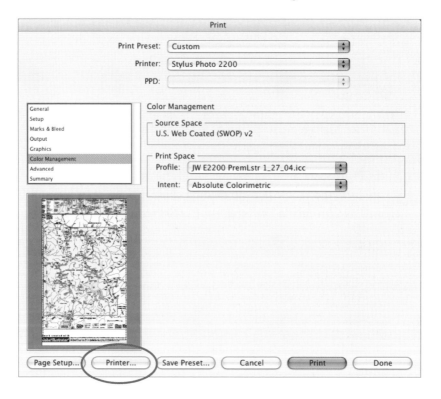

NOTE ▶ If Illustrator displays a warning dialog instructing you to set all print options in the application's own Print dialog, just click Continue.

The Mac OS X Print dialog appears.

```
                                Print
        Printer:  [ Stylus Photo 2200              [↕] ]
        Presets:  [ Standard                       [↕] ]
                  [────── Copies & Pages ──────────[↕] ]

         Copies:  [1        ]   ☑ Collated
          Pages:  ◉ All
                  ○ From:  [1        ]   to:  [1     ]

  (?)  ( Preview )  ( Save As PDF... )  ( Fax... )     ( Cancel )  ( Print )
```

7   Click the Copies & Pages pop-up menu to locate your printer's media settings, and then choose the correct paper for your device. The location of the media option varies with each printer; look for it under a heading such as Print Settings, as shown in the following figure. This is an essential step, as the media option controls the amount of ink the printer will use. If the paper you're using is not listed, either check with the paper manufacturer or choose the closest available setting. If you have the option, disable any automatic settings (such as by selecting Advanced Settings, also shown in the following figure).

```
                                Print
        Printer:  [ Stylus Photo 2200              [↕] ]
        Presets:  [ Standard                       [↕] ]
                  [────── Print Settings ──────────[↕] ]

      Page Setup:  Standard
      Media Type:  [ Premium Luster Photo Paper    [↕] ]
            Ink:   [ Color                          [↕] ]
           Mode:   ○ Automatic
                   ○ Custom
                   ◉ Advanced Settings
                   Print Quality:  [ Photo - 1440dpi  [↕] ]
                       ☑ MicroWeave
                       ☐ High Speed
                       ☐ Flip Horizontal
                       ☑ Finest Detail
```

8   Click the Copies & Pages pop-up menu again to locate your printer's color-management options, and *turn them off*. The Adobe Creative Suite applications have no way to control the color-management settings in the printer driver, so it is essential to turn off color management in the printer driver. The location of these options varies with each printer; look for them under a heading such as Custom, Advanced, or Color Management. The following image shows the Color Management option in the Epson Photo Stylus 2200 printer driver, with No Color Adjustment selected.

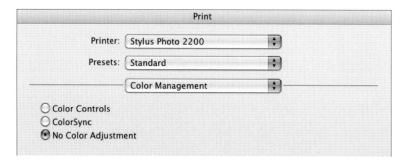

9   Click Print to return to the Illustrator Print dialog, and then click Print to begin printing. When it prints, Illustrator converts all of the color data from the source color spaces into the color space of the profile selected in the Print settings.

You can compare the print to the onscreen soft proof to see how closely they match. Keep in mind, the print may not match the screen *exactly*. It's extremely difficult to obtain a perfect match. The goal is to get a close match to gain predictability so that you can make adjustments, corrections, and separations with confidence.

Preserving Profiled Artwork in Adobe PDF

As noted earlier in this lesson, an Adobe PDF file can be used throughout the production process: as an interim comp document, as a file for soft-proofing, and as a final press or Web-ready file. There are basically three ways to create a color-managed Adobe PDF file for use in proofing and production.

First, you can click the "Save as PDF" button that appears in Mac OS X Print dialogs; second, you can save or export PDF files from Photoshop, Illustrator, InDesign, or QuarkXPress; or third, you can use Acrobat Distiller to create a PDF file from any PostScript or EPS document. All of these PDF creation methods will be covered in Lesson 9. For now, let's see how to save an Illustrator file to Adobe PDF with an embedded profile.

1   With the **Yellowstone Map.ai** sample file still open in Illustrator, choose File > Save As.

2   In the Illustrator Save As dialog, navigate to the location where you want to save the PDF file, such as in Color Management in Mac OS X Book Files > Lessons > Lesson07.

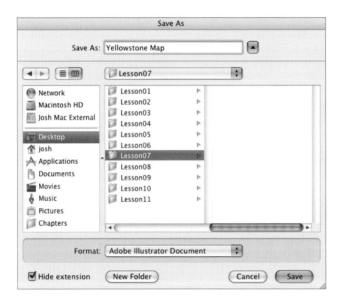

3   Choose "Adobe PDF (pdf)" from the Format pop-up menu.

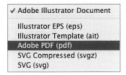

TIP ▶ Make sure the "Hide extension" box is unchecked. This appends a .pdf file extension to your new file, helping to distinguish it from the .ai version.

4 Click Save.

The Adobe PDF Options dialog appears.

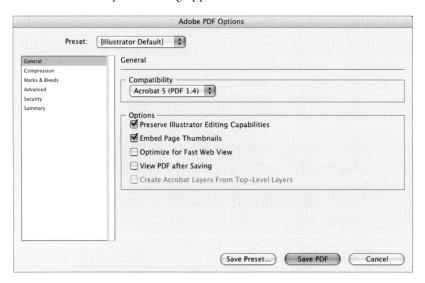

5 Choose Advanced from the list of options on the left.

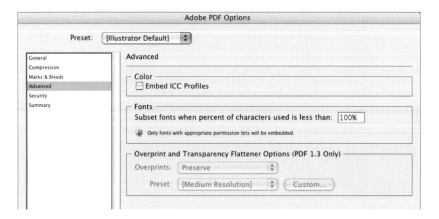

6   In the Advanced options panel, check the Embed ICC Profiles box.

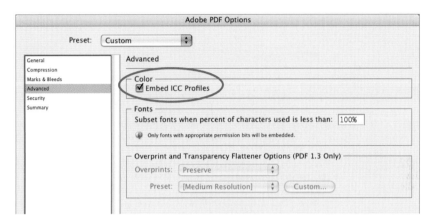

This instructs Illustrator to embed this document's source profile, which is U.S. Web Coated (SWOP) v2, in the Adobe PDF file. If the illustration contains placed art with an embedded profile, that profile will also be preserved in the PDF file. These profiles will be used by Acrobat to proof and print the PDF file.

NOTE ▶ We'll proof and print color-managed Adobe PDF files in Lesson 9.

7   Click Save PDF.

8   Press Command-Q to quit Adobe Illustrator.

What You've Learned

• You can select the same custom or preset Color Settings file in all of the Adobe Creative Suite applications, making it easy to view and print consistent color in files in Photoshop, Illustrator, InDesign, and Acrobat.

• Artwork can be tagged with profiles in Adobe Illustrator in the Missing Profiles and Assign Profiles dialogs, the same way as in Adobe Photoshop.

• You can embed profiles in PDF files that are saved from Adobe Illustrator.

8

Lesson Files
Color Management in Mac OS X Book Files > Lessons > Lesson08

Time
This lesson takes approximately 2 hours to complete.

Goals
Set up QuarkXPress for a color-managed page layout workflow

Create a document consisting of different color elements

Soft-proof the document to simulate various output devices

Use Quark CMS's utilities for color managing documents

Lesson **8**

Managing Color in Page Layout

So far, we have worked with images and artwork to improve color accuracy and predictability from creation or capture to output. In each scenario, we dealt with a single file. In reality, many creative pieces combine images, artwork, text, and other elements—each of which may have its own source color space. Color managing a document within a page layout application can be more complicated than working with a single element. Once the page is complete, it will be proofed—both onscreen and to a printer—separated for press, and/or converted for the Web. Each element on the page will be transformed from its source space to one or more output spaces.

The exercises in this lesson use QuarkXPress 6.0 to construct, proof, and print a color-managed page. While Lesson 7 covered the configuration of Adobe InDesign's Color Settings and functions, this lesson does not go into further detail about using InDesign in a color-managed environment. However, you can follow the same workflow principles described for QuarkXPress when using InDesign.

The first step is to set up the page layout application to properly handle color data. Much like Photoshop, QuarkXPress contains preference settings that determine how the application will manage color data.

Setting Up QuarkXPress's Color Preferences

Before you start this exercise, be sure that the Quark CMS XTension, which comes with QuarkXPress, is installed and enabled.

NOTE ▶ The demo version of QuarkXPress available on Quark's Web site does *not* include the Quark CMS XTension. The QuarkXPress exercises in this lesson require a full working version of QuarkXPress.

1 Launch QuarkXPress, which should be located in the Applications folder on your hard drive.

2 Choose QuarkXPress > Preferences.

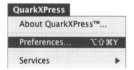

The QuarkXPress Preferences dialog appears.

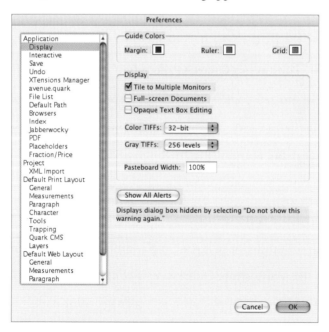

3   Choose Quark CMS from the list pane on the left.

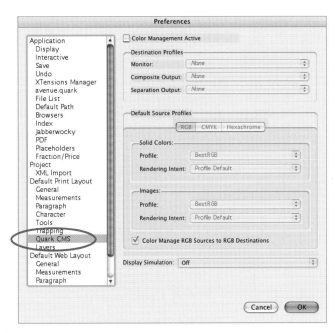

4   Check the Color Management Active box.

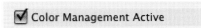

QuarkXPress's color-management preferences enable you to control which profiles are used for soft-proofing and printing, and to select a source for color data imported to and created in QuarkXPress. Initially, no Destination Profiles are selected.

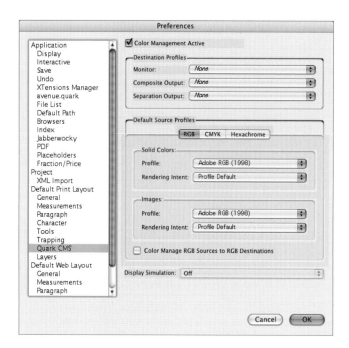

5 In the Destination Profiles area, choose a profile for your display from the Monitor pop-up menu. Choose the same profile you set in the ColorSync Preferences in Lesson 2.

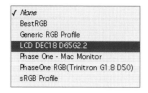

The Monitor profile will be used by QuarkXPress as the default display profile to display images and colors to the screen.

NOTE ▶ QuarkXPress does not use the ColorSync Preferences for assigning default profiles.

6   From the Composite Output pop-up menu, choose a profile for your
desktop printer.

This selection determines the default profile for the composite output
device. I have selected the custom profile for my Epson Stylus Photo 2200
that was created by Chromix.

7   From the Separation Output pop-up menu, choose a profile for your
color-separation process or device.

I have selected the U.S. Web Coated (SWOP) v2 profile, recommended by
my print provider.

NOTE ▶ Both the composite and separation output profiles can be
changed when you print from QuarkXPress.

8   Make sure the RGB tab under Default Source Profiles is selected.

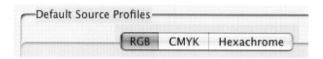

The default RGB source profiles settings determine which profiles Quark CMS will use for images and solid colors (colors defined and used in Quark) in the RGB color space.

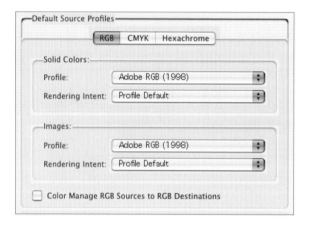

9   Under Solid Colors, make sure Adobe RGB (1998) is chosen in the Profile pop-up menu.

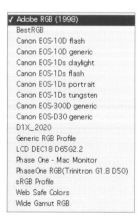

This instructs QuarkXPress to use the Adobe RGB (1998) profile for all solid colors created in the RGB color mode in QuarkXPress. Adobe RGB (1998) is a well-balanced working space and is consistent with the working space we chose in Photoshop.

10 Choose Relative Colorimetric from the Rendering Intent pop-up menu. Rendering intents determine how out-of-gamut colors are mapped into colors that are within the gamut of the output device.

11 In the Images area, make sure Adobe RGB (1998) is chosen from the Profile pop-up menu.

The Profile pop-up menu in the Images area determines the profile that will be used when RGB images that lack embedded profiles are imported into QuarkXPress. By selecting Adobe RGB (1998), we are being consistent with the way we configured Photoshop in Lesson 5 to handle images that lack embedded profiles.

When you import an image into QuarkXPress that lacks an embedded profile, you will be given the option to use the setting from the Quark CMS Preferences or to select a different profile. If you are importing an image that lacks an embedded profile, but you know the source of the data, you can choose that other profile instead of the default Adobe RGB (1998).

12 Choose Relative Colorimetric from the Rendering Intent pop-up menu. The rendering intent compares the source to the destination color space and maps out-of-gamut colors to the closest reproducible color in the destination space.

13 Check the Color Manage RGB Sources to RGB Destinations box.

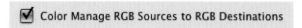

When this box is checked, QuarkXPress will color manage RGB images between their source color space and a destination color space. In order for the document's RGB images to be soft-proofed and printed to RGB composite devices such as your display and desktop printer, this option needs to be checked.

14 Click the CMYK tab under Default Source Profiles.

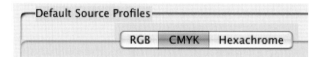

The CMYK Default Source Profiles options appear, allowing you to determine which profiles Quark CMS will use for images and solid colors (colors defined and used in Quark) in the CMYK color space.

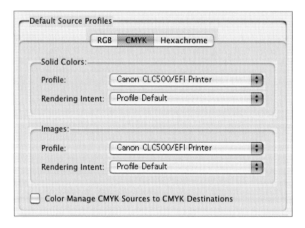

15 Under Solid Colors, choose U.S. Web Coated (SWOP) v2, or the profile
you use for separating images for press, from the Profile pop-up menu.

This instructs QuarkXPress to use the selected profile for all solid colors
created in the CMYK color mode in QuarkXPress. By using U.S. Web Coated
(SWOP) v2 profile (or the profile you use to separate data to CMYK), CMYK
colors defined in QuarkXPress will be in the color space of the printing
process. This helps ensure accurate proofing to displays using soft proofing and to composite proofing devices.

16 Set the Rendering Intent to Absolute Colorimetric, which is a good choice
for gamut mapping for solid CMYK colors.

17 Under Images, choose the profile that represents the source for CMYK images
from the Profile pop-up menu. For example, if you have a CMYK profile for
the scanner on which your images are scanned, you can use that profile.

This setting determines the default profile for CMYK images imported without embedded profiles. By selecting U.S. Web Coated (SWOP) v2 (or the profile you use for separating images for press), we are assuming that any untagged CMYK images that we receive are already separated for press.

As with importing RGB images that lack profiles, when you import a CMYK image into QuarkXPress that lacks an embedded profile, you will be given the option to use this setting from Quark CMS's Preferences or to select a different profile. So if you import an image that lacks an embedded profile, but you know the source of the data, you can select that profile instead of the default.

NOTE ▶ Quark CMS does not color manage CMYK EPS files. Working with EPS files will be covered later in this lesson.

18 Choose Relative Colorimetric from the Rendering Intent pop-up menu. This rendering intent maps out-of-gamut colors in the source profile into colors that are within the gamut of the output profile.

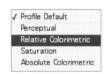

19 Check the Color Manage CMYK Sources to CMYK Destinations box.

When this box is checked, QuarkXPress will color manage CMYK images between their source CMYK color space and a destination color space that is a different CMYK space. If you want to proof the data to a CMYK printer or proofer, this option needs to be checked. Soft-proofing and printing to an RGB printer will not be affected.

NOTE ▶ QuarkXPress can also color manage the six-color Hexachrome high-fidelity color printing process. These preferences can be configured by clicking the Hexachrome tab next to the RGB and CMYK Default Source Profiles tab. If you use the Hexachrome system, consult your print provider on how to configure these settings.

20 At the bottom of the Quark CMS Preferences dialog, choose Monitor Color Space from the Display Simulation pop-up menu.

This tells QuarkXPress to use your monitor profile to display color data onscreen, which improves the accuracy of soft-proofing.

NOTE ▶ Soft-proofing in QuarkXPress will be covered in more detail later in this lesson.

21 Click OK to close QuarkXPress Preferences.

Building Color-Managed Pages in QuarkXPress

Creating page layouts often involves a variety of elements, including images, artwork, and text. Each of these may have its own color source and color space. For example, a page may contain images from a scanner (in RGB or CMYK), images from a digital camera, artwork in EPS format that is typically in CMYK, and a number of colors defined in the application that can be in RGB, CMYK, or a named color space such as Pantone.

When you're building pages, it's important that each element be accurately tagged with the source of the color data—another reason why embedding profiles is key.

In this exercise we'll build a page in QuarkXPress using several elements, ensuring all the while that each is properly color managed.

1   Launch QuarkXPress, which is located in the Applications folder on your hard drive, if it is not already open.

2   Choose File > Open and then navigate to and open the file **Sample Quark File.qxd**, located in the Color Management in Mac OS X Book Files > Lessons > Lesson08 folder on your hard drive.

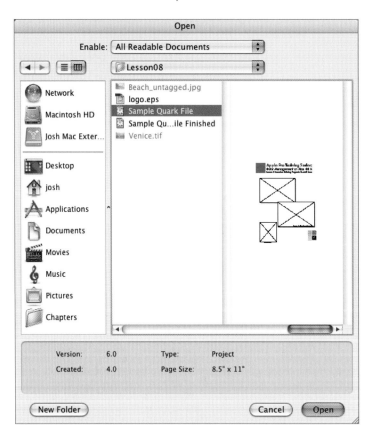

3 Click the picture box labeled Image – Venice.tif and then choose File > Get Picture.

The Get Picture dialog appears.

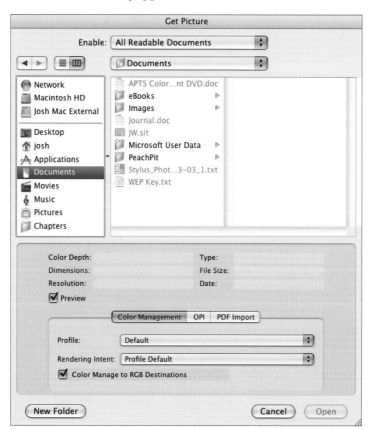

4   Navigate to and select the file **Venice.tif** in the Color Management in Mac
OS X Book Files > Lessons > Lesson08 folder on your hard drive.

When you select an image to place in a picture box, QuarkXPress displays
information about it, including whether a profile is embedded. In the case
of **Venice.tif**, the Profile pop-up menu lists Embedded (but it does not
show *which* profile is embedded). If this were incorrect, we could select a
profile from the menu.

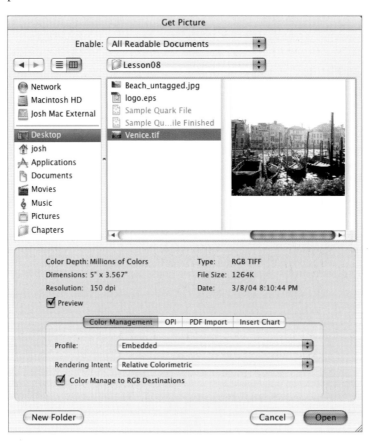

The Rendering Intent menu indicates the default rendering intent chosen in the Quark CMS Preferences. You can change it if desired by selecting a different rendering intent from the pop-up menu.

Finally, the Color Manage to RGB Destinations option is checked because we checked it in the Quark CMS Preferences. The Get Picture dialog lets you disable this command on a per-image basis, but we want to leave it checked.

5 Click Open to place the image on the page.

6 Click the picture box that is lower on the QuarkXPress page, labeled Beach_untagged.jpg, and choose File > Get Picture.

7 In the Get Picture dialog, select the file **Beach_untagged.jpg** in the Color Management in Mac OS X Book Files > Lessons > Lesson08 folder on your hard drive.

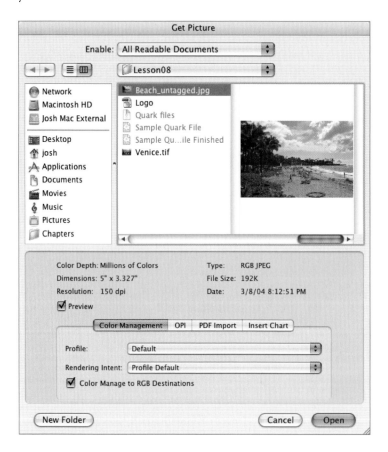

The **Beach_untagged.jpg** image does not contain an embedded profile, so QuarkXPress assigns the default profile chosen in the Quark CMS Preferences: in this case, Adobe RGB (1998).

NOTE ▶ If you are opening an untagged image and either know the source color space or wish to change the selected profile to something other than the preference, click the Profile pop-up menu and select a different profile.

8   Click Open to place the image on the page.

The onscreen representation of the images we've placed in the document have been adjusted according to the settings in the Quark CMS Preferences. The profile embedded in the **Venice.tif** image determines the source of the data, while the Quark CMS Preferences determine the profile used for the **Beach_untagged.jpg** image. The Display Simulation option, which we have set to Monitor Color Space, instructs QuarkXPress to transform any spot colors from their source color spaces to the display color space (set by the Monitor Destination Profile preference) to accurately display them.

9   Choose Window > Show Profile Information.

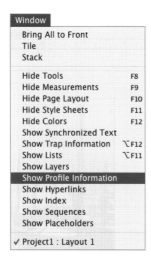

The Profile Information window appears.

10 With a selection tool, click on the **Beach_untagged.jpg** image on the page. The Show Profile Information window displays the profile information for the selected image.

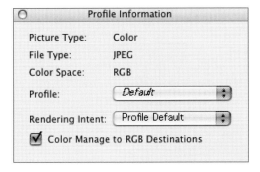

The Profile pop-up menu identifies the profile for the selected image: in this case Default is selected, as the image does not contain an embedded profile, and Quark has assigned the default profile selected in the Quark CMS Preferences. Should you desire, you could change the source profile for the image, as well as the rendering intent.

11 Choose Window > Show Colors.

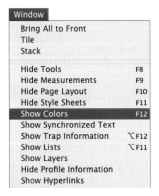

NOTE ► If the Window menu item reads Hide Colors, then the Colors palette is already open onscreen. Release the mouse without toggling the palette off.

12 Select the Image – Venice.tif text box. In the Colors palette, select the fill button (the empty rectangle) and ensure that Solid is displayed in the pop-up menu. Then choose Blue to fill the text box with blue.

13 Repeat step 12 for the Image 2 – Beach_untagged.jpg text box, filling it with Magenta.

The colors that you've selected in the Colors palette are being adjusted onscreen based on the settings in the Quark CMS Preferences. The RGB and CMYK Default Source Profiles determine the source of the data for the blue and magenta selections, respectively, while the Monitor Destination Profile determines the display profile. The Display Simulation option, which is set to Monitor Color Space, instructs QuarkXPress to transform the spot colors from their source color spaces to the display color space.

14 Click the picture box labeled Logo.eps and choose File > Get Picture.

15 Navigate to and select the file **Logo.eps** in the Color Management in Mac OS X Book Files > Lessons > Lesson08 folder on your hard drive.

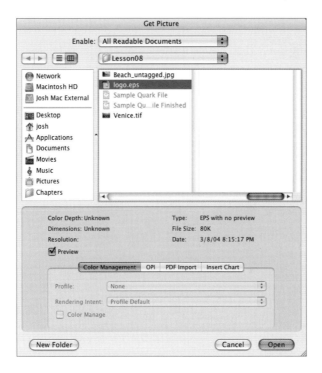

Notice that the entire Color Management area of the dialog is grayed out, and that the Profile pop-up menu reads None. QuarkXPress supports source color spaces only for images, not for vector artwork, such as EPS files. When it comes time to print, Quark CMS will convert the EPS file from the source color space to the destination space set by the PostScript Color Space Array, if any, defined in the EPS file.

16 Click Open to place the logo on the page.

17 Save the document to your hard drive, as we'll use it in the next exercise.

Soft-Proof Your Page Layout

As we saw in Lesson 6, one of the benefits of color management is the ability to soft-proof your work, to use your display to simulate the output of a printer or press. This allows you to make color adjustments onscreen, potentially reducing the number of hard proofs that you generate. In QuarkXPress (as well as in InDesign), you can soft-proof a entire page or document.

1   With the document from the previous exercise still open in QuarkXPress, choose QuarkXPress > Preferences, and then choose Quark CMS from the list pane on the left of the window.

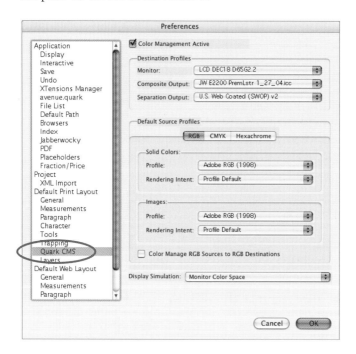

2   Click the Display Simulation pop-up menu.

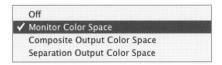

QuarkXPress supports four types of display simulations for soft-proofing:

▶   "Off" — instructs QuarkXPress to not convert any color data for the display.

▶   "Monitor Color Space," which we selected previously — instructs QuarkXPress to convert the colors in the document, including those in images, artwork (except EPS), and spot colors, from their source spaces to the display space in order to accurately display the data onscreen.

▶   "Composite Output Color Space" — simulates the printed document onscreen using the Composite Output profile selected in the Quark CMS settings. QuarkXPress will first convert color data from its source space to the color space of the printer, then to the display's, to produce a soft proof of what the document will look like on the printer.

▶   "Separation Output Color Space" — simulates the separation process onscreen, based on the Separation Output profile specified in the Quark CMS settings. QuarkXPress will first convert color data from its source space to the color space of the separation process, then to the display color space, to produce a soft-proof simulation of what the document will look like on press.

You can change this setting to see the effects onscreen. Unfortunately, there is no Preview button. You have to change the setting and close Preferences to see the effect.

3   Choose the type of simulation you want to use. For example, if you want to soft-proof the output from a press, select Separation Output Color Space. If you want to simulate the output of a desktop printer, say the Epson Stylus Photo 2200 used in previous exercises, select Composite Output Color Space.

Unless you're proofing a document to a specific output device, it's a good idea to leave Monitor Color Space as the selected simulation option. This way, any color data you work with will be adjusted for the display.

NOTE ▶ Lesson 9 covers the process of printing and proofing to output devices and separating documents for press.

4   Click OK. Quark CMS will display the Updating Picture Previews progress bar, and then redraw the document onscreen.

Page layout in monitor color space   Page layout in composite output color space

The preceding images show the differences between the Monitor Color Space and Composite Output Color Space options. The red, blue, and magenta colors will be more muted in the Composite Output Color Space, while the images will appear to have less contrast. Note that your monitor will show different colors onscreen from the printed colors in the book.

Quark CMS Utilities

The Quark CMS XTension includes two utilities that are helpful in the production of a document: Profiles Usage and the Profile Manager. Here's how
they work.

1   Choose Utilities > Usage, and in the Usage dialog that appears, click the
Profiles button.

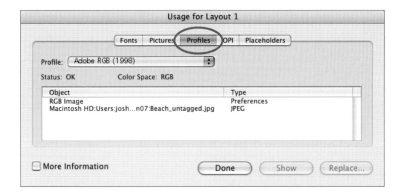

The Profiles Usage window displays all the elements in the document that
use the profile chosen in the Profile pop-up menu, such as Adobe RGB
(1998), as shown in the preceding image. It also shows the status and color
space of the selected profile.

2   Make sure Adobe RGB (1998) is chosen in the Profile menu, and then
click to select one of the objects that uses the profile.

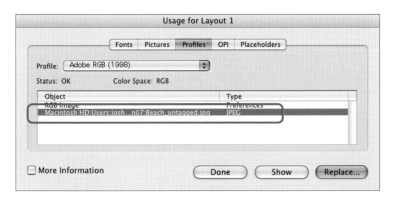

3 Click the Show button to display the elements on the page.

The Replace button in the Profiles Usage dialog allows you to change the profile for an element. This is a useful feature to ensure that all of the elements in the document are being properly color managed.

4 Click Done.

5 Choose Utilities > Profile Manager.

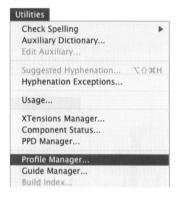

The Profile Manager window appears.

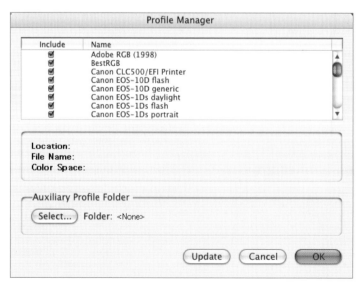

The Profile Manager lists all the profiles in the document that have been detected by Quark CMS. It also allows you to select an auxiliary profile folder. QuarkXPress does not look for profiles in all of the possible locations where profiles can be stored under Mac OS X. For example, it will not look in subfolders within the ColorSync Profiles directory. If you use QuarkXPress, therefore, you should store your profiles in the ColorSync Profiles folder itself, or use the Auxiliary Profile Folder feature to select a secondary profile location, such as Macintosh HD > Library > Application Support > Adobe > Color > Profiles.

6   Click OK to close the Profile Manager.

What You've Learned

- QuarkXPress can color manage all the elements on a page, regardless of their color spaces, except for EPS files.

- Each element in a page layout needs to have an associated profile and rendering intent.

- QuarkXPress can simulate the output of printers and printing processes onscreen, reducing the time and cost associated with creating color proofs.

- QuarkXPress's color management system includes the Profile Usage utility, which shows all of the profiles contained within a document, and the Profile Manager, which lists all of the profiles that are recognized by Quark CMS.

9

Lesson Files Color Management in Mac OS X Book Files > Lessons > Lesson09

Time This lesson takes approximately 90 minutes to complete.

Goals Print using color management to ensure consistent color through your workflow and between devices

Proof images and documents to predict the output of a particular device

Create PDF files of images, artwork, and documents

View, proof, and print PDF files with color management

Managing Color Proofs

In previous lessons we soft-proofed images, using the display to simulate the output device. This is an effective way to ensure that the color corrections you are making onscreen are accurately rendered by your output device. If the final output for your work is printed—on press, large format, or even short run—you will need to make a hard-copy proof at some point.

Conventional press proofing media, such as Matchprint or other high-end contract proofs, can be very expensive and time consuming to produce, and they may not be the best option for types of printing other than offset. Today's desktop printers offer excellent quality and wide gamuts—wide enough that they make excellent proofing devices. While prints from a desktop or large-format printer may not entirely replace contract proofs, they can be made quickly and easily, and with color management they can come close to those from the final output device.

One of the most significant, and least touted, advantages to color management is the ability to reproduce color consistently across devices—from soft-proofing on the display to proofing on desktop printers to the final output on press or from photo printers—all from a single unmodified file. You only need to select the device, and color management performs the necessary conversion. This is a much easier workflow than what was once required.

The concept of a proof is to simulate the final output device, such as a printing press (represented by a profile for the particular type of printing process) on a desktop printer. Adobe Photoshop can perform simulation for images, while Adobe InDesign and QuarkXPress can perform simulation for entire pages.

Once you are satisfied with the proof, the next step is to prepare the data for the final output device or devices, as the case may be. In this lesson, we'll cover the process of printing and proofing images and pages, as well as learn how to use PDF as a proofing tool.

Proofing from Adobe Photoshop

Adobe Photoshop can simulate what an image will look like when it is output by a printer by using either the display (soft-proofing) or another printer (proofing or cross-rendering). Proofing an image in Photoshop makes use of the Proof Setup and printing functions, both of which we learned in previous exercises; all that you need to do now is to tell Photoshop which device you want to simulate.

> **NOTE ▶** Before starting this exercise, make sure Photoshop's Color Settings are configured according to the exercises in Lesson 5.

1   Launch Photoshop by double-clicking its application name or icon in the Applications folder of your hard drive, or by clicking it in the Dock.

2   Choose File > Open, navigate to Color Management in Mac OS X Book Files > Lessons > Lesson09, and open the **Soaps.jpg** file.

NOTE ▶ If you have set Photoshop's RGB working space to a profile other than Adobe RGB (1998), the Photoshop Embedded Profile Mismatch dialog will appear when you open the file. In that case, select the "Convert document's colors to the working space" option, and then click OK.

3   Choose View > Proof Setup > Custom.

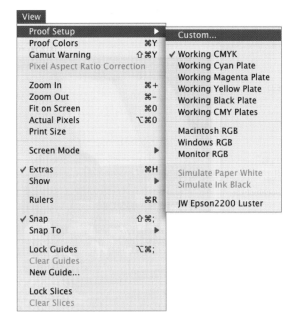

The Proof Setup dialog appears.

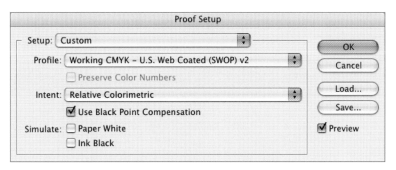

4   Choose a press profile from the Profile pop-up menu, such as U.S. Web Coated (SWOP) v2 in my example.

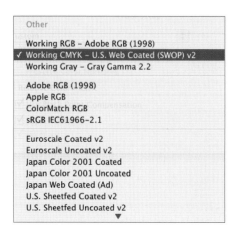

5   If Preserve Color Numbers is available, deselect it.

If you select a profile that is in the same color mode as the document's working space, the Preserve Color Numbers option becomes available. The **Soaps.jpg** image is an RGB image; the U.S. Web Coated (SWOP) v2 profile is CMYK; therefore the option is not available.

6   Choose Intent > Relative Colorimetric.

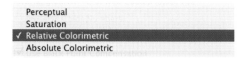

The rendering intent determines how colors that are out of gamut for the selected device are mapped to a color within the device's gamut. Relative Colorimetric, which is suitable for photographic images, compares the highlight of the source color space with that of the destination color space and shifts out-of-gamut colors to the closest reproducible color in the destination color space. It preserves more of the original colors in an image than the Perceptual intent.

7   Make sure Use Black Point Compensation is checked. This instructs Photoshop to use the entire dynamic range within the profile.

> **TIP** Check the Preview box to immediately see the effect of a selection on the image.

8   If it's available, check Simulate Paper White. When Simulate Paper White is selected, Simulate Ink Back is automatically selected and grayed out. These options, which are not supported by all profiles, improve the accuracy of your soft proof.

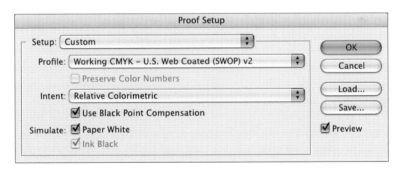

9   Click OK to close the Proof Setup dialog and then press Command-Y to toggle the soft proof off and on.

Now that you can see the soft proof, let's print a color-managed hard proof.

10 Choose File > Page Setup.

11 Select your printer from the "Format for" pop-up menu.

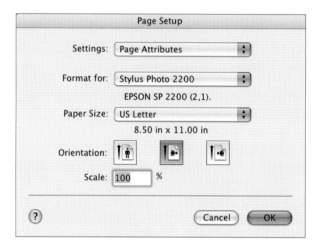

12 Confirm that Paper Size is set to US Letter (or the equivalent for your device), that the Orientation is set to landscape, and that Scale is 100%, as shown in the preceding image.

13 Click OK.

14 Choose File > Print with Preview.

15 In the Photoshop Print dialog that appears, check the Show More Options box and select Color Management from the pop-up menu just below it.

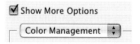

16 Under Source Space, select Proof: Proof Setup: U.S. Web Coated (SWOP) v2.

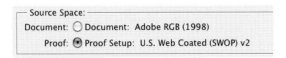

This tells Photoshop to use the Proof Setup space, in this case U.S. Web Coated (SWOP) v2, as the source print space for the image.

NOTE ▶ To change the device you are simulating, you must change the selected profile in Proof Setup, as demonstrated in the beginning of this exercise.

17 Under Print Space, choose the profile for your printer from the Profile pop-up menu.

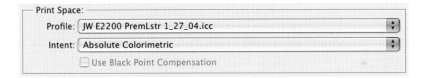

This setup tells Photoshop to color manage the file from the working space, Adobe RGB (1998), to the Proof Setup space, U.S. Web Coated (SWOP) v2, to the printer-profile space, which in this example is the custom Epson Stylus Photo 2200 that I created in Lesson 3. In other words, we're telling Photoshop to simulate on the Epson Stylus Photo 2200 what the image will look like printed on a press using U.S. Web Coated (SWOP) v2.

TIP ▶ Keep in mind that the proof may not be an exact match due to differences in the device gamuts, whiteness of the paper stock, and reproduction characteristics of each device. You can use the ColorSync Utility to compare the U.S. Web Coated (SWOP) v2 and Epson Stylus Photo 2200 profiles and see how the color spaces of the two devices correspond.

Photoshop automatically changes the Intent to Absolute Colorimetric, and Use Black Point Compensation is disabled.

The following image illustrates the correct setup of the Print dialog to proof U.S. Web Coated (SWOP) v2 on the Epson Stylus Photo 2200.

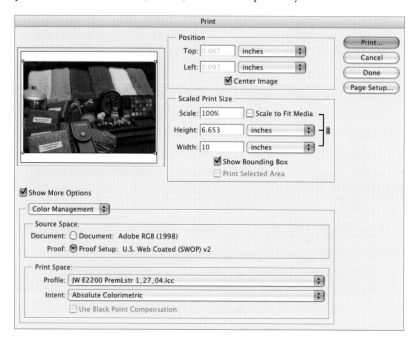

18 Click Print.

19 In the Print driver dialog that appears, choose your printer from the Printer pop-up menu.

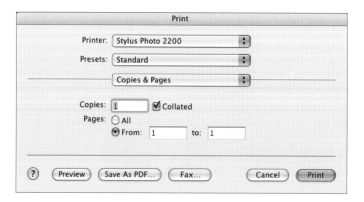

20 Click the Copies & Pages pop-up menu to locate your printer's media settings, and then choose the correct paper for your device. The location of
the media option varies with each printer; look for it under a heading
such as Print Settings. The following image shows the Epson Print Settings
menu, with Premium Luster Photo Paper chosen from the Media Type
pop-up menu. If you can, disable any automatic settings. For example, I
chose Advanced Settings, also shown in the following screen shot, instead
of Automatic.

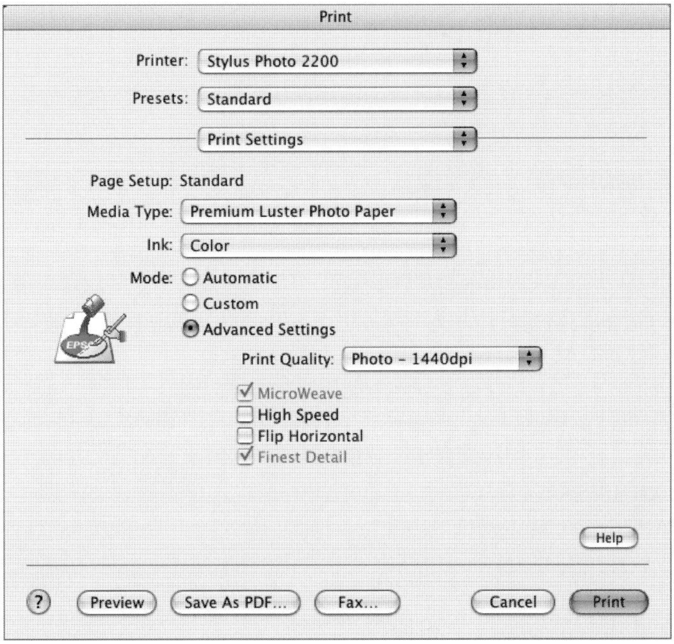

21   Click the Copies & Pages pop-up menu again to locate your printer's color-management options and *turn them off.* The location of these options varies with each printer; look for them under a heading such as Custom, Advanced, or Color Management. The following image shows the Color Management option in the Epson Stylus Photo 2200 printer driver, with No Color Adjustment selected.

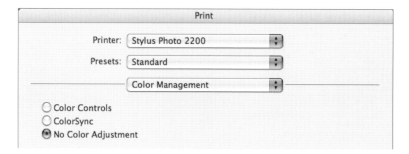

22   Click Print to start printing. When the print is finished, you can compare it with the onscreen soft proof. Make sure your Proof Setup is set to the final output device.

Photoshop handles proofing and printing of image data. To proof and ultimately print designs that incorporate multiple types of elements, you will need to use a page layout application such as QuarkXPress or InDesign. Both of these applications include the ability to proof and separate a page layout using color management.

Proofing from QuarkXPress

Undoubtedly, if you design color-managed pages in QuarkXPress you're going to want to create hard-copy proofs. We'll learn how to do that now, but before we start, be aware that QuarkXPress supports printing with color management only when the printer is a PostScript or PostScript-compatible device. If your printer is not PostScript compatible, see the section later in this lesson on how to create PDF files for instructions on proofing QuarkXPress documents to non-PostScript printers. There are third-party PostScript RIPs available for non-PostScript-compatible printers, such as the Epson Stylus Photo 2200.

NOTE ▶ PostScript includes its own color-management capabilities. As this is an advanced and complex topic, we have chosen to focus on applying color management on the Mac, and not in the printer.

1   Launch QuarkXPress by double-clicking its application name or icon in the Applications folder of your hard drive, or by clicking it in the Dock.

2   Choose File > Open and then navigate to and open the file **Sample Quark File Finished.qxd**, located in the Color Management in Mac OS X Book Files > Lessons > Lesson09 folder on your hard drive.

NOTE ▶ If QuarkXPress prompts you that the links to the images in the document are broken, you can locate the files in the Color Management in Mac OS X Book Files > Lessons > Lesson08 folder on your hard drive.

3   Choose File > Print.

4   In the QuarkXPress Print dialog that appears, click the Profiles tab.

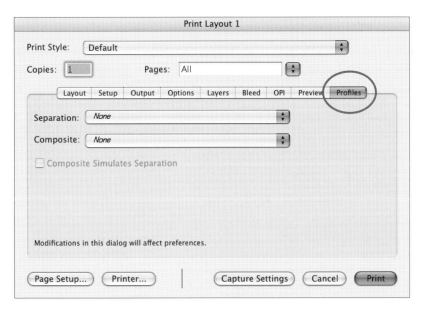

There are three proofing controls in the Profiles tab of the QuarkXPress Print dialog:

▶ Separation — allows you to select a CMYK profile for separations. All color data will be converted from its source color space to the selected profile, and then separated into grayscale files representing data for CMYK (or even more inks, depending on the profile). Separations are actually enabled in the Layout tab of the Print dialog.

▶ Composite — allows you to select a profile for printing the document to a PostScript printer or proofing system. All color data will be converted from its source color space to the selected profile.

▶ Composite Simulates Separation — instructs QuarkXPress to simulate the Separation device on the Composite device. For example, if you wanted to proof on a desktop printer what the document would look like on press, you would first select the press profile under Separations, then select the profile for your desktop printer under Composite, and finally check the Composite Simulates Separation box.

5 Choose U.S. Web Coated (SWOP) v2 (or the profile you use to separate your documents for press) from the Separation pop-up menu.

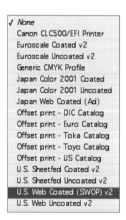

6 Choose the profile for your desktop printer or proofing device from the Composite pop-up menu.

I have selected a custom profile for my HP DeskJet 800 series desktop
PostScript printer, which I use for proofing.

7   If you want to see a proof of what the document will look like when separated for press, check the Composite Simulates Separation box. Keep in
mind that the proof may not be exact, depending on the differences in
gamut between your desktop printer and the press profile used for press.

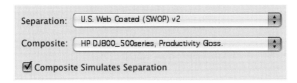

8   Click the Printer button.

9   Follow steps 19 through 21 of the previous exercise to choose your media
and to disable color management in your printer driver. When you're done,
click Print to return to the QuarkXPress Print dialog, and then click Print
to start printing.

> **NOTE** ▸ If QuarkXPress displays a warning when you go to the OS X
> Print dialog, just click OK.

In the next exercise, we'll create, proof, and print PDF files. If your desktop
printer is not PostScript compatible, you can use a PDF file to proof QuarkXPress
documents with color management.

Creating Color-Managed PDF Files

The PDF file format is a flexible way of sending your documents to others as comps, soft and hard-copy proofs, and as final production files, all without the recipient's needing to have the source application and associated elements such as images and fonts. The PDF file is essentially a proof of your document, but it is a very flexible proof from a color-management perspective. Much like a QuarkXPress or InDesign document, a PDF document can contain multiple objects, including images, vector artwork, and text. Each object in a PDF document can be in a different color space and can be tagged with a profile, as long as the file type of each embedded element supports profile embedding or tagging. In Adobe Acrobat 6.0 Professional, the file can be soft-proofed, printed to a hard-copy proof, or separated for press via Adobe's Common Color Architecture controls in much the same way as it can in Photoshop. Once you know how to create a color-managed PDF file, you can send it to clients, prepress providers, and printers with the assurance that the color in your document will be accurate.

There are three basic ways to create a PDF file from a document:

- Print to PDF using the Mac OS X printer driver. You can create a PDF file from virtually any file by clicking Save as PDF in the Mac OS X Print dialog. This is a good way to quickly create PDF files, but this option lacks the advanced controls required for converting complex color documents such as page layouts.

- Save as or export to PDF. Adobe Photoshop and Adobe Illustrator allow you to save individual images and vector artwork as PDF files. InDesign and QuarkXPress let you convert documents with multiple elements to PDF by using a Save or Export command.

- Use Acrobat Distiller. This method uses the creation application's color-management capabilities in the same way as when a document is printed from that application, except that the document is output to an electronic file rather than to a hard copy. Acrobat Distiller then converts the file into PDF, including embedded profiles for each element on the page. This is the best method for converting complex documents to PDF in a color-managed workflow when the application doesn't support saving files as PDF.

Creating PDF Files Using the Mac OS X Printing System

Any document in any Mac OS X application can be converted to PDF by using the Mac OS X printing system. This method basically uses the PDF 1.4 specification, but it does not let you customize the conversion process in any way. So if the application you're using does not support color management, such as any application in the Microsoft Office suite, the resulting PDF file will not have embedded profiles.

1   Launch Microsoft Word by double-clicking its application name or icon in the Applications folder of your hard drive, or by clicking it in the Dock.

2   Choose File > Open, navigate to Color Management in Mac OS X Book Files > Lessons > Lesson09, and open the **Word Sample.doc** file.

3   Choose File > Print.

4   In the Print dialog that appears, click Save as PDF.

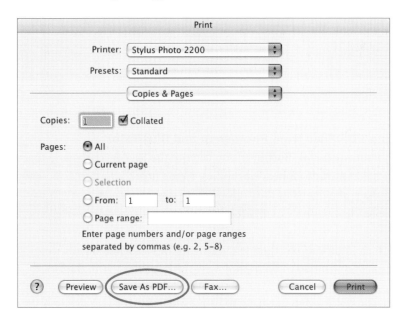

5   In the Save to File dialog, enter a different filename and/or location if desired, and click the Save button.

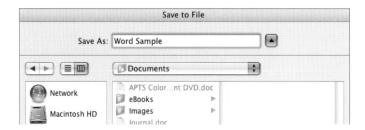

The document is saved as a PDF file.

6   Open the resulting PDF file in Acrobat Reader or Professional.

Since Microsoft Word does not support color management, the **Soaps.jpg** image is not tagged with a profile. Acrobat will apply color-management policies (which we'll set later in this lesson) and use the default RGB working-space profile for this image. However, unlike QuarkXPress or InDesign, Acrobat does not allow you to assign a specific profile to the image.

NOTE ▶ Users can also apply a Quartz Filter at print time to generate PDF files.

Creating PDF Files from Photoshop and Illustrator

Within Photoshop and Illustrator, you can use the Save As command to create PDF files that include embedded profiles. Here's how to do it in Photoshop; the process is analogous in Illustrator. Before starting, make sure you have configured Photoshop's Color Settings as described in Lesson 5.

1   Launch Photoshop by double-clicking its application name or icon in the Applications folder of your hard drive, or by clicking it in the Dock.

2   Choose File > Open, navigate to Color Management in Mac OS X Book Files > Lessons > Lesson09, and open the **Soaps.jpg** file.

NOTE ► If you have set Photoshop's RGB working space to a profile other than Adobe RGB (1998), the Photoshop Embedded Profile Mismatch dialog will appear when you open the file. In that case, select the "Convert document's colors to the working space" option, and then click OK.

Photoshop can save RGB, indexed-color, CMYK, grayscale, bitmap-mode, Lab color, and duotone images in PDF. Our **Soaps.jpg** file is RGB, so there's no problem.

3 Choose File > Save As. The Save As dialog appears.

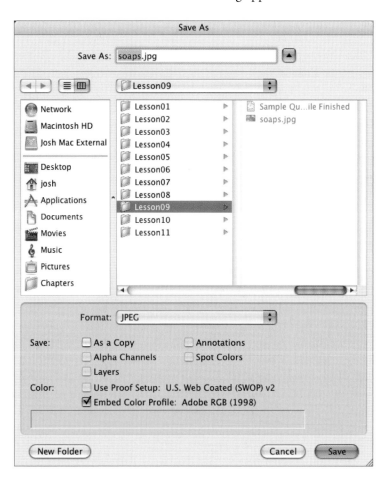

4 Choose Format > Photoshop PDF.

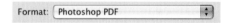

The Photoshop PDF format can contain only a single image—the image being saved. A second PDF format supported by other applications, Generic PDF, can contain multiple pages and images.

5 Make sure the Embed Color Profile box is checked. This instructs Photoshop to embed the document working-space profile—in this case, Adobe RGB (1998)—in the PDF file.

6 Leave the Use Proof Setup box unchecked. Checking it instructs Photoshop to convert the image from its working space to the profile selected in the Proof Setup—in this case, U.S. Web Coated (SWOP) v2—before saving as a PDF file. You would check this option if you wanted to send the image to someone only for the purpose of proofing it to the selected output device.

7 Click Save. The PDF Options dialog appears.

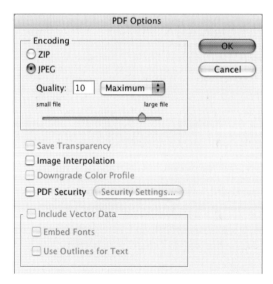

All of the default settings in the PDF Options dialog should be fine for our PDF. The Downgrade Color Profile option, which is grayed out in the preceding image, is enabled when the embedded profile is an ICC version 4 profile. When checked, it converts the embedded profile to an ICC version 2 profile, which can be useful when working with older applications that do not support the version 4 profile specification.

8   Click OK to save the image as a PDF file. When the image is opened in Acrobat, the embedded profile, Adobe RGB (1998) in this case, will be used as the source profile and will be color managed to the display using the display profile as the destination.

9   Close the image and press Command-Q to quit Photoshop.

> **NOTE ▶** See Lesson 7 for an exercise saving vector artwork as a PDF file from Illustrator.

Creating PDF Files from QuarkXPress

QuarkXPress provides two ways to produce color-managed PDF files. The first is to use QuarkXPress's built-in PDF engine to convert the documents to PDF. This is essentially similar to saving the document as a PDF file, and it is easy and effective.

The second method is to convert the document to a PostScript file, which will be converted into PDF by Acrobat Distiller. This method provides finer control over the conversion process, but requires you to have Acrobat Distiller.

Both methods provide similar control over color management in the process of converting to PDF, as we'll see in this exercise.

1   Launch QuarkXPress by double-clicking its application name or icon in the Applications folder of your hard drive, or by clicking it in the Dock.

2   Choose File > Open, navigate to Color Management in Mac OS X Book Files > Lessons > Lesson09, and open the **Sample Quark File Finished.qxd** file.

3   Choose QuarkXPress > Preferences. The Preferences dialog appears.

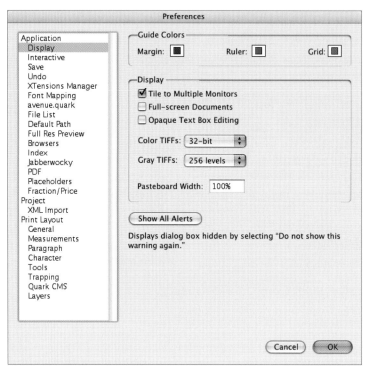

4   Click PDF in the list of Application options on the left.

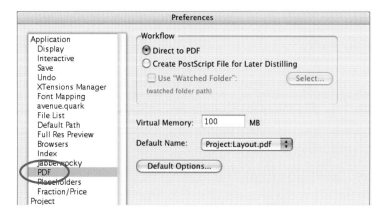

QuarkXPress provides two conversion options: Direct to PDF instructs QuarkXPress to convert the document directly to PDF using its built-in conversion option. Create PostScript File for Later Distilling instructs QuarkXPress to create a PostScript file from the document, which can then be converted to PDF using Acrobat Distiller (which we'll do later in this lesson).

5   Select Direct to PDF, and click OK to close the Preferences dialog.

6   Choose File > Export > Layout as PDF.

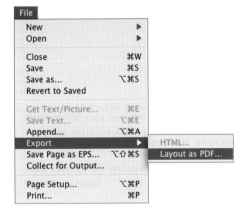

7   In the Export as PDF dialog that appears, click the Options button.

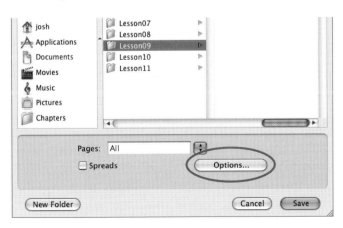

8   In the PDF Export Options dialog that appears, click the Output tab.

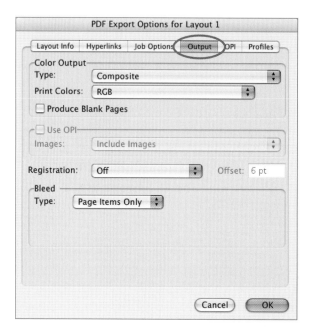

This tab includes controls for converting color data in QuarkXPress documents to PDF.

9   In the Color Output area, choose Type > Composite.

This tells QuarkXPress to create a composite PDF document instead of a separated file with individual grayscale pages for each press plate.

Each time color data is converted between device profiles and color spaces, some data is lost. Therefore, you should convert data as few times as possible. The preferred workflow is to create a composite PDF file from your QuarkXPress document and separate it for press in Acrobat. This way you use the same file for both the composite proof and the color separations for press, and the color data is converted only once—at output.

10 Choose the appropriate color space of your document from the Print Colors pop-up menu. In our example, that's RGB.

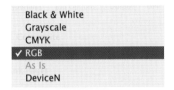

Choosing RGB instructs QuarkXPress to convert all the elements in the document from their native color spaces—including RGB color spaces— to the specific gamut of the RGB profile selected in the Profiles tab.

If you're working in a CMYK document, choosing CMYK instructs QuarkXPress to convert all the elements from their native color spaces to CMYK using the CMYK profile selected in the Profiles tab. Documents already in CMYK will be converted from their native color spaces to the CMYK profile selected in the Profiles tab of the PDF Export Options dialog.

If you have a mixture of RGB and CMYK elements, consider selecting RGB as the document color mode. When you convert color data from RGB to CMYK, color data is lost. If you intend to output to more than one device or to an RGB printer, it is better to leave RGB objects in RGB when the PDF file is created.

The menu offers other options as well:

▶ Black & White — instructs QuarkXPress to convert all elements to black and white (1-bit color). Most monochrome printers include internal algorithms for converting color data to black and white, which are likely to produce better results for that particular device than this option.

▶ Grayscale — instructs QuarkXPress to convert all elements to grayscale (8-bit color). Most monochrome printers include internal algorithms for converting color data to grayscale, which are likely to produce better results for that particular device than this option.

▶ As Is — leaves the color data alone during the PDF conversion process. It also strips out any embedded or tagged profiles. If you want to convert the document to PDF without any color management or conversion, select this option (you must first disable the Quark CMS XTension to use this option).

▶ DeviceN — uses the Separations profile selected in the Profiles tab to produce files for in-RIP separations and for multi-ink separations such as Hexachrome.

11 Click the Profiles tab.

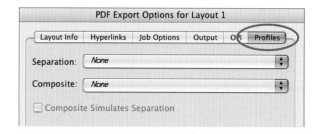

This tab lets you specify which profiles are used when the document is converted to PDF, and the options are similar to those found in the Profiles tab of QuarkXPress's Print dialog: There are Separation and Composite pop-up menus and a Composite Simulates Separation check box.

12 Leave the Separation and Composite pop-up menus set to None.

The Separation pop-up menu determines which profile is used when the QuarkXPress document is converted to PDF as a single file with one grayscale page for each press color. The Composite pop-up menu determines which profile is used when the QuarkXPress document is converted to PDF as a single, composite file.

QuarkXPress will convert everything on the page from its source color space to the destination space (or spaces, if you select Composite Simulates Separation), *except* for EPS and PDF files. QuarkXPress does not color manage these file types.

By selecting None, you're telling QuarkXPress to leave everything in its source—or tagged—space *unless it's in a different color space than the option selected in the Output tab of the PDF Export Options dialog*. For example, in the Output tab, if you select RGB in Print Colors, the **Venice.tif** and **Beach_untagged.jpg** files will be left in their respective color spaces during the PDF conversion process.

However, if you select CMYK in Print Colors, the **Venice.tif** and **Beach_untagged.jpg** files will be converted to the CMYK color space during the PDF conversion process. Unfortunately, this conversion is done using an internal QuarkXPress algorithm and does not use Quark CMS or ICC profiles.

The best option is to use images that are all in the same color space, and select that as the color mode of the document (in step 10 of this exercise). EPS files will be passed through without conversion; color elements created in QuarkXPress can be tagged with a working-space profile in the same color mode as the document. Using the **Sample Quark File Finished.qxd** as an example, select RGB for the document color mode and leave the Separation and Composite profile options set to None:

▶   The **Venice.tif** image is tagged with Adobe RGB (1998) and will be converted to PDF with the embedded profile preserved.

▶   The **Beach_untagged.jpg** image has been tagged within QuarkXPress with Adobe RGB (1998) and will be converted to PDF with the tagged profile preserved. If it were not tagged, the default RGB working-space profile selected in the Quark CMS preferences would be applied. We set this to Adobe RGB (1998) in Lesson 8.

▶   The **Logo.eps** file will be passed through untouched, and its embedded profile (a CMYK profile) will be preserved.

▶   The red and green colors selected in the text boxes will be tagged with the RGB working-space profile, which will be preserved during the conversion.

The benefit of keeping as much color data in the same working space is consistency between applications, and fewer color transformations.

NOTE ▶ With None selected, the Composite Simulates Separation box is unchecked and unavailable. When it is checked, however, the color data in the resulting PDF file will be converted to simulate the Separation device on the Composite device.

13 Click OK to close the PDF Export Options dialog.

14 Click Save to convert the file to PDF.

Creating a PostScript File

The following method is useful if you have existing PDF conversion workflows or settings for Acrobat Distiller.

1 With QuarkXPress still open from the previous exercise, choose QuarkXPress > Preferences, and click PDF in the list of Application options on the left.

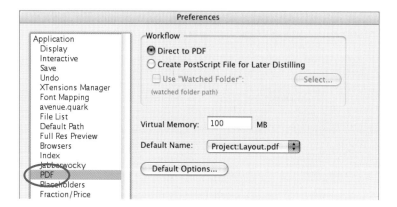

2 Click the Create PostScript File for Later Distilling radio button, and then click OK to close QuarkXPress's Preferences.

3   Repeat steps 6–14 of the previous exercise. When you save the file, you will
     be saving a PostScript file, which we'll convert to PDF in the next exercise.

4   Press Command-Q to quit QuarkXPress.

Creating Color-Managed PDF Files Using Acrobat Distiller

Acrobat Distiller, which is a component of Adobe Acrobat 6.0 Professional,
provides advanced controls and greater workflow flexibility over the conversion of documents to PDF. To use Distiller, you first print your document
from its originating application, such as QuarkXPress, to a PostScript or EPS
file rather than to an output device. If the application supports color management—if it tags the file and its components with embedded profiles—Distiller
will include those tags in the resulting PDF file just as if you'd printed it with
color management to an actual printer.

How color data is converted from the source document to the PDF document
depends on the how the color-management preferences are set in Distiller.
Distiller uses the same Color Settings file as the rest of the Adobe Creative Suite,
but you configure it a bit differently. In this exercise, we'll apply the Color
Settings file we created in Photoshop to Distiller's Acrobat PDF Settings, and
then we'll create a PDF file from the QuarkXPress document that we printed
to a PostScript file in the previous exercise.

1   Launch Acrobat Distiller by double-clicking its application name or icon
     in the Applications > Acrobat 6.0 Professional folder of your hard drive, or
     by clicking it in the Dock.

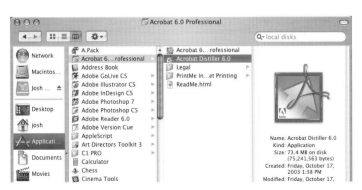

The Acrobat Distiller window appears.

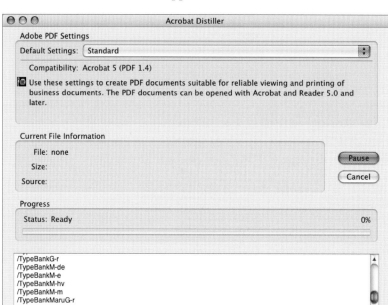

2   Click on the Default Settings pop-up menu to see a list of PDF Settings files.

Acrobat Distiller uses a PDF Settings file to control how the conversion is made. Settings specify, for example, whether and how fonts are embedded, whether and how images are compressed, and whether and how color management is applied. Distiller ships with six preset Default Settings, which range from Smallest File Size (suitable for PDF files destined for the Web) to PDFX1a and PDFX3, which are ISO standards for compliance with specific prepress characteristics, including support for ICC profiles. Let's start from the High Quality PDF setting to create a custom Settings file that supports color management.

3   Choose Default Settings > High Quality.

4   Choose Settings > Edit Adobe PDF Settings.

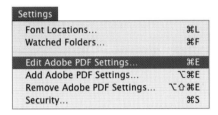

5   In the Adobe PDF Settings dialog that appears, click the Color tab.

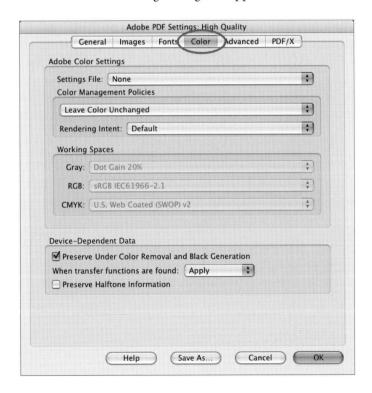

The Color panel of the Adobe PDF Settings dialog contains settings similar to those in the Color Settings dialogs in Photoshop, Illustrator, and InDesign CS.

6   From the Settings File pop-up menu, choose the Color Settings file that you created in Photoshop in Lesson 5, which you've also chosen in Illustrator, InDesign, and Acrobat Professional.

Settings File: Josh Photo Workflow

The Adobe Color Settings are updated to reflect these new preferences.

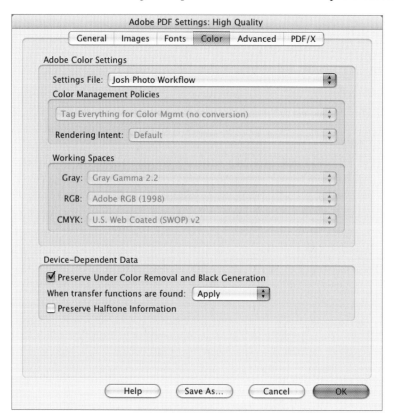

By using the same Color Settings file across all Adobe Creative Suite applications, you ensure that color management is handled consistently between them.

Notice that when you choose a Settings File, the Color Management Policies and Working Spaces are grayed out. You cannot change these options in Distiller. If you want to create custom Adobe Color Settings, you would leave the Settings File set at None.

NOTE ▶ Custom policies created by choosing None cannot be saved for use in other Creative Suite applications. Use this option only when you need to convert a particular file using a unique setting.

Although Distiller's Color Settings policies are similar to those in other Adobe applications, they function slightly differently.

The four policies are:

▶ "Leave Color Unchanged" — does not change the color values during the conversion process and does not embed profiles in the PDF file. This setting can be used in a tightly calibrated closed-loop environment where color is managed "by the numbers."

▶ "Tag Everything for Color Mgmt (no conversion)" — tags all objects with working-space profiles unless they contain embedded profiles. These profiles are used as the source color spaces when the PDF file is proofed or printed. No color conversion is performed during PDF file creation. This is the ideal option if you want to create a PDF file that can be used as a comp, soft proof, or proof, or to generate separations (which we'll cover later in this lesson), and it was chosen in my custom photo workflow.

▶ "Tag Only Images for Color Mgmt (no conversion)" — works the same as Tag Everything, except that only images are tagged. All other elements are untagged.

▶ "Convert All Colors to sRGB" — converts all color values to the sRGB space using embedded and working-space profiles as the source of the data. Although sRGB is a device-independent color space, it is not large enough to be useful for printing. This option is useful when the PDF file will be used on the Web.

The Rendering Intent option determines how out-of-gamut colors will be mapped during the PDF conversion process. This option can be overridden by the selection of a rendering intent in the Print dialog of an application.

The Gray, RGB, and CMYK Working Spaces selections are the profiles that will be used when an object lacks an embedded profile. By using the same Color Settings file across all Adobe applications, all untagged data is consistently tagged with working-space profiles.

7 Accept the default options in the Device-Dependent Data area. These options, which we didn't see in Photoshop, Illustrator, or InDesign, determine how data that is already in the color space of a particular device is converted. These options do not apply to objects tagged with ICC profiles, but they will apply to EPS files.

8 Click OK to close the Adobe PDF Settings dialog. Acrobat Distiller prompts you to save them.

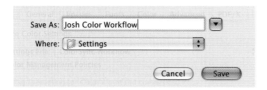

9 Name your new Adobe PDF Settings file and save it to the default location: Macintosh HD > Users > Shared > Adobe PDF 6.0 > Settings.

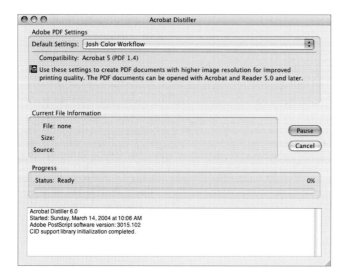

Congratulations! You now have a custom Adobe PDF Settings configuration that applies color management to your Distilled Adobe PDF files in a manner consistent with other Adobe Creative Suite applications. The new settings are chosen in Distiller's Default Settings menu and will be used to create your next PDF file. Now we're ready to distill a PDF file from the QuarkXPress file we printed to PostScript in the previous exercise.

TIP If you also create lower-quality PDF files, such as for use on the Web, customize the Smallest File Size PDF Settings file in Distiller. For the Web, you may want to use sRGB rather than Adobe RGB (1998) as the RGB working-space profile.

10 Choose File > Open.

11 Navigate to the **Sample Quark File Finished.ps** file we created earlier in this lesson when we printed the sample Quark document to a file, and click Open.

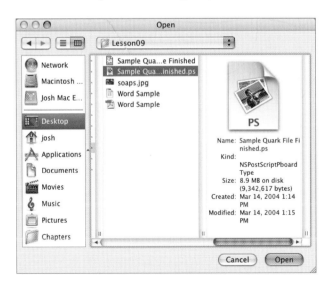

Acrobat Distiller converts the file. The resulting PDF is saved to the same directory as the source file.

12 Press Command-Q to quit Acrobat Distiller.

Proofing and Printing Color-Managed PDF Files

You can use Acrobat Professional to view, soft-proof, print, and separate PDF files much in the same way you performed similar color-management functions in Photoshop.

Acrobat Professional uses ColorSync to determine the display profile. When a PDF file is opened, Acrobat Professional automatically color manages the PDF to the display, using the embedded profile as the source color space and the display profile as the destination. Let's see how to use Acrobat to soft-proof the PDF file we created earlier in this lesson by saving it from QuarkXPress.

NOTE ▶ Before you start this exercise, make sure you have configured Acrobat's Color Settings according to the exercise in Lesson 7.

1 Launch Acrobat 6.0 Professional by double-clicking its application name or icon in the Applications folder of your hard drive, or by clicking it in the Dock.

2 Choose File > Open and navigate to the **Sample Quark File Finished.pdf** document that we created earlier in this lesson. Click Open.

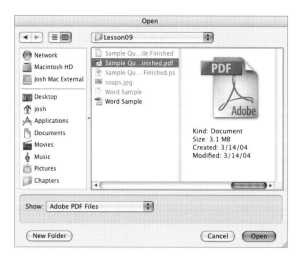

3   Choose Advanced > Proof Setup > Custom.

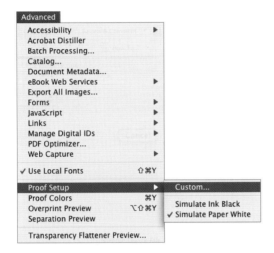

The Proof Setup dialog appears.

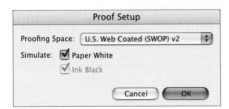

4   In the Proofing Space pop-up menu, choose the profile for the output
device that you wish to soft-proof. For example, I chose U.S. Web Coated
(SWOP) v2 to simulate what the document will look like on press.

5   If the Simulate Paper White option is available, check it. Selecting this
option automatically selects the Ink Black option. These options are not
available with all profiles.

6   Click OK to close Proof Setup. Acrobat automatically turns on soft-proofing.

7   Choose Advanced > Proof Colors or press Command-Y a few times to toggle the soft proof off and on to see the differences.

Now that you've viewed a soft proof in Acrobat, let's print a hard-copy proof.

8   Choose File > Print.

9 In the Acrobat Print dialog that appears, choose your printer from the Printer pop-up menu, and then click the Advanced button.

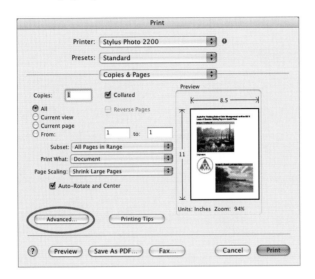

The Advanced Print Setup dialog appears.

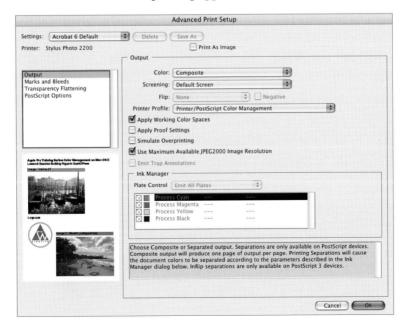

The Advanced Print Setup dialog lets you control how Acrobat Professional applies color management to the PDF file at print time.

10 Click the Color pop-up menu.

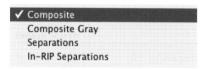

There are four Color options, which control the type of color conversion Acrobat Professional will apply during print time.

▶   Composite — instructs Acrobat Professional to print the document as a composite file.

▶   Composite Gray — instructs Acrobat Professional to print the document as a composite grayscale file.

▶   Separations — instructs Acrobat Professional to separate the document into the color space selected in Acrobat Professional's Color Settings dialog, which is U.S. Web Coated (SWOP) v2 in our example, and to produce one grayscale page for each color. This option is available only for PostScript or PostScript-compatible devices.

▶   In-RIP Separations — sends a composite file to the output device (presumably an imagesetter, platesetter, or digital press) with instructions on how to separate the colors. This option is available only for PostScript 3 or PostScript 3–compatible devices.

11 If you are printing to a desktop printer or composite proofer, as in the case of my Epson Stylus Photo 2200, select Composite. If you were making separations, you would select the appropriate option for your output workflow.

12 Choose a profile for your output device from the Printer Profile pop-up menu. For example, I chose the custom profile for my Epson that I created in Lesson 3.

Printer Profile: JW E2200 PremLstr 1_27_04.icc

All color data will be converted from its source color space to the output-profile color space during printing. If you were performing separations, you would select the appropriate printing-process profile, such as U.S. Web Coated (SWOP) v2.

You may notice that there are two non-device-specific options that appear in the Printer Profile pop-up menu: Same as Source (No Color Management) and Printer/PostScript Color Management.

Same as Source (No Color Management) instructs Acrobat Professional to send the file to the printer without color management. Embedded profiles are not used; the color values in the file are sent to the printer without conversion.

Printer/PostScript Color Management instructs Acrobat Professional to convert embedded and output ICC profiles into PostScript color-management commands. These are embedded in the data sent to a PostScript printer. When the printer interprets the file, the commands instruct it to apply color management in the printer. This option applies only to PostScript printers.

13 Check the Apply Working Color Spaces box.

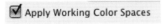

This option instructs Acrobat Professional to use the working-space profiles as the source color-space profiles for untagged color objects in the document. There is no reason to not use this option.

14 If you want to simulate the output of one device on another, check the Apply Proof Settings box.

☐ Apply Proof Settings

When Apply Proof Settings is checked, Acrobat Professional will use the output profile selected in the Proof Setup as the device to be simulated, and the output profile selected in the Printer Profile pop-up menu as the output device where the file will be printed. I don't want to simulate the Proof Setup, so I'm leaving this box unchecked.

15 Click OK to close the Advanced Print Setup dialog and return to the main Acrobat Print dialog.

16 Click the Copies & Pages pop-up menu to locate your printer's media settings, and then choose the correct paper for your device. The location of the media option varies with each printer; look for it under a heading such as Print Settings. In addition, if you can, disable any automatic settings, such as by choosing Advanced Settings instead.

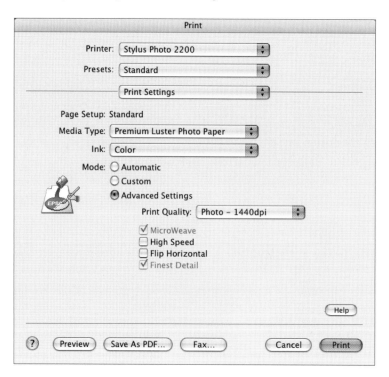

17 Click the Copies & Pages pop-up menu again to locate your printer's color-management options and *turn them off*. The location of these options varies with each printer; look for them under a heading such as Custom, Advanced, or Color Management. The following image shows the Color Management option in the Epson Stylus Photo 2200 printer driver, with No Color Adjustment selected.

18 Click Print.

NOTE ▶ The Adobe Acrobat Reader does not support color management.

As you have seen, the PDF file format provides powerful proofing capabilities from a single self-contained file. The key to generating high-quality PDF proofs is in successfully generating the PDF. As described in this lesson, the best approach is to create the PDF without converting color data to output-device-specific color, but rather keeping it in a working space such as Adobe RGB. This will ensure the highest-quality conversion for proofing, printing, and separating.

What You've Learned

- Color management enables you to proof images and documents to output devices, as well as simulate one output device on another. Properly setting up the application's preferences and printing options will ensure smoother and more predictable color output.

- When converting documents to PDF, color data can either be left in its color space or converted to another color space for proofing or simulation. In either case, profiles are associated with each element on the page.

- There are multiple ways to create PDF files including saving them or exporting them from an application, or using Acrobat Distiller to create them from PostScript files. Acrobat either preserves the color data in its color space or preserves embedded profiles.

- Composite PDF files can be soft-proofed, proofed, and separated for press using color management to ensure consistent color.

10

Lesson Files Color Management in Mac OS X Book Files > Lessons > Lesson10

Time This lesson takes approximately 90 minutes to complete.

Goals Configure ImagePrint color-management settings

Print images from ImagePrint using a color-managed output workflow

Lesson 10
Color Server Workflows

In previous lessons, we have printed color documents using an application's color-management features. Among the benefits of this approach is that a single file can be output to any device for which you have a profile.

In some workflows, however, it makes sense to apply color management elsewhere. For example, the application you are using may not support color management, or you may want more control over the printing process.

One type of application that provides advanced features and workflow enhancements for printing is a RIP, or raster image processor. RIPs convert image data into a format that is understood by a printer, and they usually have features not found in design applications.

In this lesson, we'll print images with color management using a RIP. Applying color management in a RIP isn't necessarily better than applying it in a design application—it depends on your workflow and on whether you will benefit from the additional features of a RIP.

Applying in-RIP Color Management

Software RIPs are specialized printer drivers that replace the driver that is installed with your printer. They take input from applications and convert, or rasterize, the information into data that the printer understands so that it can put dots on a page. Software RIPs typically offer features that are not found in standard printer drivers. For example, they often offer advanced queue management, network printing, tone and gradation control, selective color adjustment, PostScript or PDF support, and the ability to create hot folders for automated processing.

ColorByte Software's ImagePrint is an example of such a software RIP. In addition to the features mentioned above, it also supports the use of ICC color profiles for screen-to-print and print-to-print matching. Multiple images can be placed on a page and color managed individually.

ImagePrint 6.0 supports Epson Stylus Photo, Roland, Fuji Pictrography and certain HP printers, and it includes profiles for various combinations of paper, ink, and viewing conditions. It also supports working with custom profiles. The following exercises demonstrate how to apply color management in a software RIP using ImagePrint. A trial version of ImagePrint is available on the company's Web site, www.colorbytesoftware.com. If you use a different software RIP, look for comparable commands and functions in that application.

> **NOTE** ▶ If you haven't downloaded and installed the trial version of ImagePrint, do so now before continuing this lesson.

Configuring Your Printer

The first step is to configure ImagePrint to work with your printer.

1   Launch IP Install, located in the Applications > ImagePrint folder of your
hard drive, by double-clicking its application name or icon.

The IP Install dialog appears.

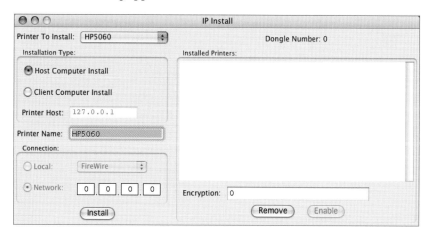

One of the ways that ImagePrint enhances output is by providing its own printer driver, which replaces the manufacturer's driver. IP Install configures the RIP software for your printer—more precisely, for the printer model and the type of connection to your Mac.

2   Choose your printer from the Printer To Install pop-up menu. For example, I chose the Epson Stylus Photo 2200.

3   Under Installation Type, select Host Computer Install.

ImagePrint supports network printer sharing. First you must install Image-Print on the same computer to which the printer is connected, known as the Host Computer. Then, if you want to print to the printer from other computers, you would install ImagePrint on those computers using the Client Computer Install feature.

4   ImagePrint enters a default name for the printer, such as Epson2200. If you wish, enter a different name for your printer.

Printer Name: Epson2200

5 From the Connection Local pop-up menu, choose the type of connection
that links your printer to your Mac.

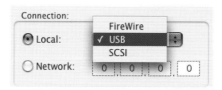

6 Click the Install button.

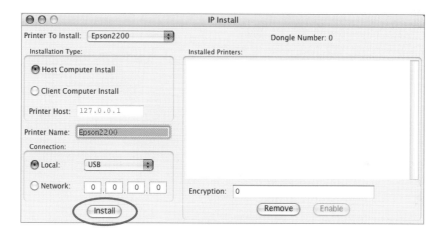

ImagePrint installs its printer driver on your computer. When finished, it
alerts you that the installation has been completed successfully.

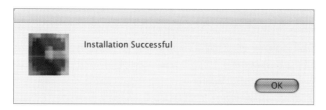

7 Click OK to close the Installation Successful dialog.

The ImagePrint printer driver is now installed for your printer, and your printer appears in the Installed Printers list box.

NOTE ▶ If you have purchased a license for ImagePrint, you would enter your encryption code in the Encryption field at the bottom of the dialog.

8 Press Command-Q to quit IP Install.

Configuring ImagePrint's Color-Management Preferences

Now that the printer is installed, the next step is to configure ImagePrint's color-management preferences.

1 Launch ImagePrint, located in the Applications > ImagePrint folder on your hard drive, by double-clicking its application name or icon.

2 Choose Image > Color Management.

The Color Management dialog appears, open to the Output tab.

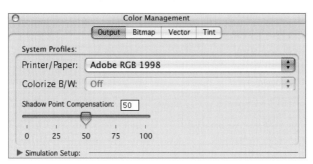

3   Click the Printer/Paper pop-up menu.

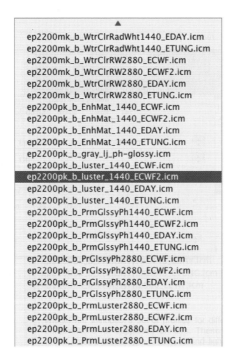

ImagePrint includes a large set of profiles for many ink-and-paper combinations for supported printers. The profile names indicate the printer model, paper type, ink type, and lighting conditions. Some profiles also include specific color spaces, such as grayscale.

4   Choose a profile for your printer, ink, and paper combination. For example, I chose ep2200pk_b_luster_1440_ECWF2.icm. This indicates a profile for the Epson Stylus Photo 2200 with photo black ink, premium luster paper, a printing resolution of 1440 dpi, and viewing conditions of mixed fluorescent and cool-white incandescent lighting. Unless you have a custom profile for your printer, I recommend starting with the ECWF2 set of profiles; these profiles represent the mixed cool-white and fluorescent lighting typically found in homes and offices. If, however, you're viewing prints in a color-correct light box, select a profile ending in EDAY, which represents daylight.

NOTE ▶ ImagePrint looks for profiles in its own directory. If you have custom printer profiles, install them in Macintosh HD > Applications > ImagePrint > Color.

One of the benefits of ImagePrint is its ability to print color-managed grayscale images. ImagePrint includes several grayscale profiles, such as Ep2200UCMGrayEMatte1440.icm. If you select a grayscale profile in the Printer/Paper pop-up menu, the Colorize B/W menu becomes active. This menu is used when you want to print a color image as grayscale.

NOTE ▶ In Mac OS X, all profiles end with the .icc or .pf suffix. On Windows, however, the default suffix is .icm. Both operating systems recognize profiles ending in .icc and .icm. ImagePrint has chosen to ship profiles ending in .icm.

5   If you want to bring out shadow detail in your print, increase the amount of Shadow Point Compensation. I recommend leaving it at the default of 50 and making adjustments based on your prints.

Shadow Point Compensation is similar to the Use Black Point Compensation option in Photoshop, except that ImagePrint enables you to control how much compensation is applied.

6   Click the triangle at the bottom of the dialog to toggle open the
Simulation Setup area.

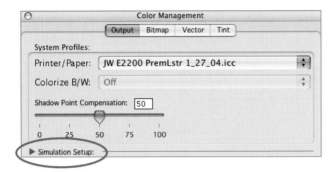

This is where ImagePrint lets you enable device simulation, or the
capability to predict what the output of one device will look like
on another.

If you wanted to simulate the output of a device or printing process,
such as U.S. Web Coated SWOP v2, on your printer, you would choose
that profile from the Proofer pop-up menu. For now, let's leave the
Proofer menu set at None.

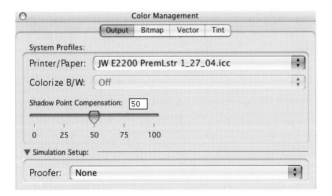

7 Click the Bitmap tab at the top of the Color Management dialog.

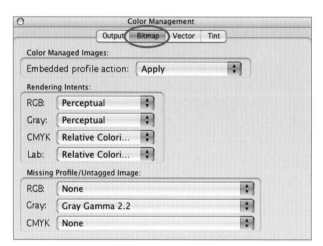

The settings in the Bitmap tab are similar to Photoshop's Color Settings preferences in that they set the default behavior for embedded profiles, rendering intents, and missing profiles.

8 Make sure Apply is chosen from the "Embedded profile action" pop-up menu.

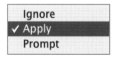

The "Embedded profile action" menu determines how ImagePrint manages images with embedded profiles:

▶ Ignore — instructs ImagePrint to ignore profiles embedded in images and to use the profile selected as the default for the image type.

▶ Apply — instructs ImagePrint to use profiles embedded in images, and is the recommended setting.

NOTE ▶ If you're working with a particular image for which you do not want to use the embedded profile, either change it in Photoshop or change this preference in ImagePrint before opening the file.

▶ Prompt — instructs ImagePrint to ask you if you want to use the embedded profile, or to ignore it and use the default profile for the image type.

9 Chose a rendering intent for each image color mode.

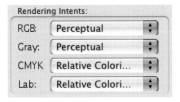

ImagePrint recommends Perceptual rendering for images and Absolute Colorimetric for simulation. In previous lessons in this book, we have used Relative Colorimetric for images, but there is no single correct choice. The best option is to experiment and then determine which setting works best for you.

10 In the Missing Profile/Untagged Image area, specify how you want ImagePrint to handle RGB, CMYK, and grayscale images that do not have embedded profiles.

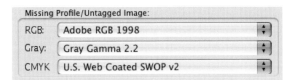

I recommend using the same settings as in Photoshop, as shown in the preceding image: Choosing RGB > Adobe RGB 1998 instructs ImagePrint to use Adobe RGB 1998 as the default working space for all RGB images that lack profiles. This setting will also be used for RGB images when the embedded-profiles option is set to Ignore.

Choosing Gray > Gray Gamma 2.2 instructs ImagePrint to use Gray Gamma 2.2 as the default working space for all grayscale images that lack profiles. This setting will also be used for grayscale images when the embedded-profiles option is set to Ignore.

Choosing CMYK > U.S. Web Coated SWOP v2 (or your preferred CMYK profile) instructs ImagePrint to use U.S. Web Coated SWOP v2 (or your preferred CMYK profile) as the default working space for all CMYK images that lack profiles.

11 Now click the Vector tab at the top of the Color Management dialog.

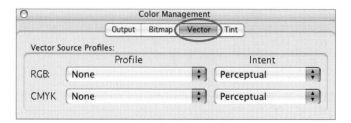

The settings in the Vector tab specify the default behavior for working with vector artwork, such as Adobe Illustrator and EPS files. They also determine the default profile and rendering intent to use when opening RGB or CMYK vector artwork that lacks embedded profiles.

12 Choose RGB > Adobe RGB 1998 and choose Relative Colorimetric for the corresponding Intent.

13 Choose CMYK > U.S. Web Coated SWOP v2 (or your preferred CMYK working-space profile) and choose Absolute Colorimetric for the corresponding rendering Intent.

ImagePrint's Color Management preferences are now configured. You do not need to close the Color Management preferences dialog—you can leave it open onscreen and change the settings depending on the particular image you are printing. This is how the Color Management window is meant to be used.

Printing from ImagePrint

ImagePrint enables you to lay out images and artwork on a page for printing. In this exercise, we'll place an image on a page, which will be color managed by the settings established in the previous exercise, and then we'll print it.

1   With ImagePrint still open on your Mac, choose File > Open.

2   Navigate to and open the sample file **Venice.tif**, located in the Color Management in Mac OS X Book Files > Lessons > Lesson10 folder of your hard drive.

The Venice image opens in ImagePrint.

The black outline shows the printable area of the page, with the image placed in it. The image can be moved around on the page, and other images can be added. Each image on a page can have its own source profile. ImagePrint will convert each image from its source color space to the output space selected in the printer profile.

Like Photoshop, ImagePrint always displays images with display correction. The image data is converted from the source color space to the display space for viewing—the data in the file is not actually changed.

3   Make sure your Printer, Page, Quality, and other printer setup menus (at the top of the window) are configured correctly for your output device.

The Quality selection allows you to choose the quality at which the print will be made from a list of those supported by the currently selected printer. This is different from the resolution of the image. Printers such as the Epson Stylus Photo 2200 use output resolution as a measure of quality; 2880 is the highest quality. Select the resolution at which you normally print images.

NOTE ► This setting should match the profile selected in the previous exercise.

4   Choose File > Print.

5   In the Print Dialog window that appears, give your job a name, and then click the Setup button.

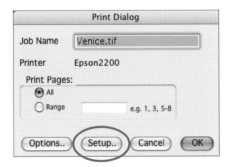

The Printer Setup dialog provides additional output controls for your printer.

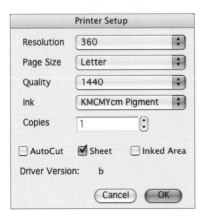

6   Choose Resolution > 180 dpi.

   NOTE ▶ The Page Size and Quality settings are the ones we chose in the document page's Printer Setup area.

7   If your printer supports multiple ink sets, choose the type of ink you're using for this job.

8   Click OK to begin printing. ImagePrint will convert the image data from the image's embedded profile to the destination profile selected in the Color Management dialog, which in this case is ep2200pk_b_luster_1440_ECWF2.icm, a custom profile for the Epson Stylus Photo 2200 provided by ColorByte.

9   Print the image again on different paper, or at a different resolution, selecting the corresponding profile. Then place your own images on the page and print using the same procedures.

   When you have a few printouts, compare them to each other and to the screen. The ImagePrint soft proof should provide results comparable to soft proofs in Photoshop.

The standard version of ImagePrint supports the printing of most image and vector (EPS) files. If you want to print QuarkXPress, InDesign, or PDF documents, you will need the ImagePrint PostScript option. With the PostScript option, you would build color-managed pages following the same approach described in Lesson 8. When you are ready to output the file, instruct the application to not color manage the file when printing. (In the QuarkXPress Print dialog, select None for the Composite and Separation profile selection. In Adobe applications, select Printer Color Management in the printer profile pop-up menu, which appears in different locations in each Adobe application.) ImagePrint will then convert all elements on the page(s) from their source color spaces to the destination color space specified in its Color Management settings. Untagged elements will be managed by the missing-profile policies.

What You've Learned

- Software RIPs provide advanced controls over the printing process, bypassing the manufacturer's printer driver.

- ImagePrint supports advanced color-management features such as adjustable shadow-point compensation, color-managed grayscale printing, and soft-proofing.

- ImagePrint's Color Management settings control how it displays, prints, and color manages images. Properly setting up color management in ImagePrint will ensure smoother and more predictable color output.

11

Lesson Files   Color Management in Mac OS X Book Files > Lessons > Lesson11

Time   This lesson takes approximately 60 minutes to complete.

Goals   Soft-proof images for the Web and digital video

Color manage images for the Web and digital video

Use color management in a Web browser to view images

Color manage QuickTime videos in preparation for streaming over the Internet

Internet and DV Color Management

When creating and producing color content, it's always a good idea to think ahead about all of the possible media for your work. In previous lessons, we've focused on print as the final destination. In reality, most content created today is also destined for the Web and in some cases digital video (DV) as well. You can easily manage color to these output media just as you do to a printing device.

The Internet is a wonderful medium for distributing content to a large number of viewers. The majority of design and imaging applications support Internet formats, making it easy to create content for both print and the Web. However, the Internet presents some significant challenges when it comes to color management, as does digital video. When you print a color document, you know that each print is going to be consistent. First, you use color management to communicate the color intent to your prepress and print partners, and then the press operator uses process controls to keep the color consistent throughout the press run.

With the Internet and video, you can still communicate your intent, but there is less guarantee that the recipients—those surfing the Web and watching digital video—will see the color you intended. The challenge with preparing color for the Internet and for digital video is that the quality of the medium—the viewer's computer display or television set—is unpredictable. Outside of imaging and publishing professionals and advanced hobbyists, very few computer displays are calibrated, and even fewer are configured for color management. Televisions on which viewers may watch a digital video aren't calibrated at all. This essentially means that each Web surfer and TV viewer may see different colors on the display or screen. To use color management for these output media, you can apply the techniques we learned in earlier lessons, to minimize unpredictability when publishing your color content to the Internet and digital video.

Understanding sRGB

Until now, we have avoided using the sRGB profile because it has a limited color gamut and is not suitable for a print-based workflow. sRGB is, however, appropriate for display-based media, as it is fairly representative of the average PC display in use. Indeed, the sRGB color space was created by HP and Microsoft to be representative of the average PC display used by most people. When you realize that most people's displays are not calibrated, or even set to a white point other than the manufacturer's default, it's easy to understand why sRGB is a smaller color space than those used in creative applications.

To illustrate the size and shape of the sRGB gamut, you can use the ColorSync Utility to compare sRGB with other color spaces, as we learned in Lesson 1. But let me save you the trouble: The following images show the sRGB gamut (in color) compared with the Adobe RGB (1998) gamut (in white). Notice how much less color is contained in the sRGB color space.

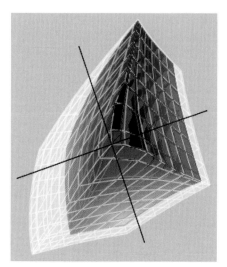 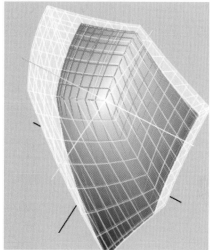

Because sRGB is a small color space, it's best to use a larger space, such as Adobe RGB (1998) to edit your images. However, when you want to see how those images will look when they're on a Web page, you can use the sRGB profile to soft-proof your color content in Photoshop.

> **NOTE** ▶ If you are creating color exclusively for the Internet, you should consider using sRGB as your working-space profile within applications such as Adobe Photoshop.

Soft-Proofing for the Web and Digital Video

Here's how to soft-proof a color image for the Web and for video color spaces.

> **NOTE** ▶ Before starting this exercise, make sure Photoshop's Color Settings are configured according to the exercises in Lesson 5.

1 Launch Adobe Photoshop by double-clicking its application name or icon in the Applications folder of your hard drive, or by clicking it in the Dock.

2 Choose File > Open, navigate to Color Management in Mac OS X Book Files > Lessons > Lesson11, and open the **Soaps.jpg** file.

NOTE ▶ If you have set Photoshop's RGB working space to a profile other than Adobe RGB (1998), the Photoshop Embedded Profile Mismatch dialog will appear when you open the file; select the "Convert document's colors to the working space" option, and then click OK.

3 Choose View > Proof Setup > Custom.

The Proof Setup dialog appears.

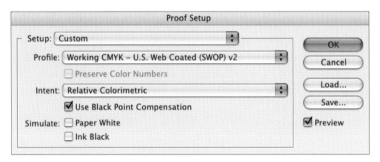

First, we'll soft-proof for the Web using the sRGB profile.

4 Choose sRGB from the Profile pop-up menu.

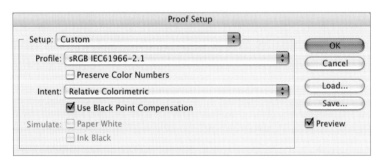

5 Check the Preserve Color Numbers box.

☑ Preserve Color Numbers

Preserve Color Numbers tells Photoshop to simulate how the image will look without converting colors from the document space to the proof-profile space. It simulates color shifts that may occur when the image's color values are interpreted using the proof profile instead of the document profile. In addition, checking Preserve Color Numbers disables all other options in the dialog, defaulting to Relative Colorimetric as the rendering intent (because that's selected in Color Settings).

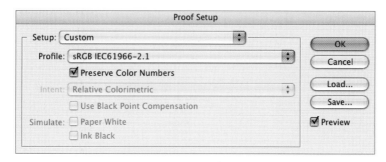

6   Click OK to see the soft proof.

Now let's see a soft proof of the image for video output. This is useful, for example, if the image will be composited as a background into a digital video.

7   Choose View > Proof Setup > Custom.

8   From the Profile pop-up menu, choose either NTSC (1953) or PAL/SECAM. If HDTV is the target destination, sRGB is also a good choice.

NTSC (1953) is the North American video standard. PAL/SECAM is used in the rest of the world.

9   Again, check Preserve Color Numbers.

10 Click OK to view the soft proof.

That's all there is to it. You can also perform soft proofs for illustrations and page layouts using the Proof Setup feature in Illustrator, InDesign, and Acrobat Professional.

Preparing Files for the Web and Digital Video

Most Web browsers, televisions, DVD players, and the like, do not support ICC color management and would not know what to do with an embedded profile. The best way to prepare your files for use on the Web and in digital video is to actually convert the color data from its working color space to the target color space after you've edited it. For example, if you intend to post an image to a Web site, convert it to sRGB and embed the profile in the image. This ensures that the file is in the correct color space for the medium, and that the profile will be used by any color-management-aware application. For example, Adobe GoLive supports color management in that it recognizes and embeds profiles in images.

1 Make sure the **Soaps.jpg** image is still open in Photoshop.

2 Check the information area in the lower left of the image window. It should read Adobe RGB (1998).

3   If the information area displays something different, such as the currently selected tool or the size of the document, choose Document Profile from the pop-up menu right next to it.

4   Choose Image > Mode > Convert to Profile.

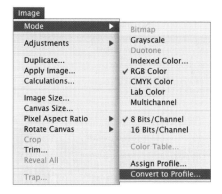

The Convert to Profile dialog appears.

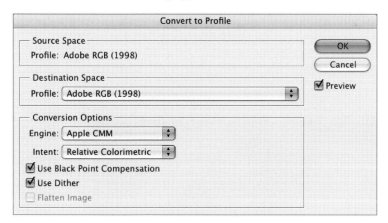

Convert to Profile enables you to convert an image from the embedded document profile space, listed under Source Space, to another profile space, listed under Destination Space. If the image doesn't have a profile, Photoshop will use the working space as the source space.

This feature is useful for converting images from one color space to another, such as separating images for press. It provides greater control over the conversion process than making a color-mode change. You can, for example, more easily change the destination space and the conversion options. In contrast, Photoshop's mode-change commands (such as Image > Mode > CMYK, or Image > Mode > RGB) use the Preferences in Color Settings; if you want to change the destination space, you have to change the Preferences.

The Engine, Intent, Use Black Point Compensation, and Use Dither conversion options in the Convert to Profile dialog are the same as those in the Color Settings dialog, which were described in detail in Lesson 5. The Flatten Image setting is used to flatten the layers of an image upon conversion, and it is only active when the image has multiple layers.

5   Since our destination in this example is the Web, choose Destination Space Profile > sRGB.

6   Toggle the Preview option off and on to see the changes.

7   Click OK to convert the image's color space to sRGB and to embed the sRGB profile.

The image is now in the sRGB working space, converted from Adobe RGB (1998). Note that the information area now displays sRGB as the embedded profile.

8   Choose File > Save for Web. The Save for Web dialog appears.

9   Choose JPEG from the file format pop-up menu.

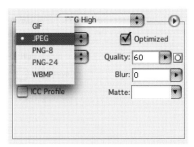

10 When JPEG is selected as the file format, the ICC Profile check box becomes available. Check it now.

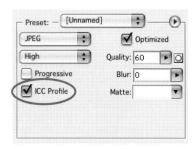

This instructs Photoshop to embed the current working-space profile, sRGB in this case, into the image file.

NOTE ▶ Photoshop's Save and Save As dialogs also allow you to embed the working-space profile, and in those dialogs, this option is checked by default.

11 Click Save.

12 In the Save Optimized As dialog that appears, change the filename to **Soaps_srgb.jpg**, and click Save again.

13 Press Command-Q to quit Photoshop.

Now, when the image is placed into an HTML page, it will already be in the best color space for the Web—sRGB. Additionally, it has an embedded profile, so in the event that the image is viewed by a color-management-savvy Web browser, the colors will be adjusted for that system's display.

If the destination for the image is digital video—say you are going to composite it into a Final Cut Pro scene—you will want to choose NTSC (1953) in step 5 of this exercise to convert the image's profile to an industry-standard destination profile suitable for video output in the United States. Then you simply save the file using the Save As command, give it a new name so that you know it is the video version of the image, and make sure the Embed Color Profile box is checked in the Save As dialog.

Color Management in Web Browsers

In an ideal world, Web browsers would recognize embedded profiles in images and artwork and manage their color accordingly. Well, the world is almost perfect.

Both Apple Safari and Microsoft Internet Explorer for the Mac (version 5.5) support ColorSync for displaying JPEG images with color management; Netscape Navigator does not. Thus, if you apply color management to the JPEG images that you create for the Web, viewers using two out of three of the most popular Web browsers on Panther should see managed color. I say "should" because in Internet Explorer, you can actually turn color management off. In Safari, it is always on. And for both browsers, ColorSync support applies only to JPEG images. The GIF file format, which is commonly used for graphics and vector artwork published on the Web, does not support ICC profiles.

Safari and Internet Explorer tap into color management in the same way: When loading JPEG images, they look for embedded profiles. If a profile is detected, the color is matched from the embedded profile to the display profile, which is set in the Display Preferences.

So although color-management support is limited on the Web, it's worth doing an exercise so that you can see the difference it makes when it is applied.

1   Launch Safari by double-clicking its application name or icon in the Applications folder of your hard drive, or by clicking it in the Dock.

2   Choose File > Open File, navigate to Color Management in Mac OS X Book Files > Lessons > Lesson11, and open **Soaps.jpg**.

3 Now choose File > Open File, navigate to the same folder, and open **Soaps_untagged.jpg**.

Safari opens each image in its own window. Position the two images side by side.

4   Study the differences. The colors are more saturated in the image that has
    the embedded sRGB profile. This should be most noticeable in the figurine
    soaps in the foreground, and in the towels in the background.

    NOTE ▶ The differences may be subtle, depending on the particular image.

Color Managing QuickTime Videos with ColorSync

You can use QuickTime Pro to apply color management to QuickTime movies.
This is useful for preparing movies for display on different devices, as well as
on the Internet. This exercise requires not only QuickTime Pro, which unlocks
the functionality we need in QuickTime Player, but also a sample QuickTime
file. If you don't have one of your own, go to www.apple.com/quicktime and
download a movie trailer or other sample file before you start. For example,
I downloaded and used an iPod ad.

1   Launch QuickTime Player by double-clicking its application name or icon
    in the Applications folder of your hard drive, or by clicking it in the Dock.

2   Choose File > Open Movie in New Player, select a QuickTime file, and
    click Open.

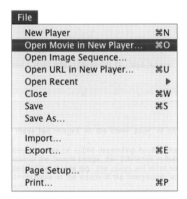

Color management is applied when the QuickTime video is exported, so
let's do that now.

3   Choose File > Export.

4   In the "Save exported file as" dialog that appears, choose Export > Movie to QuickTime Movie. Then click the Options button to open the Movie Settings dialog.

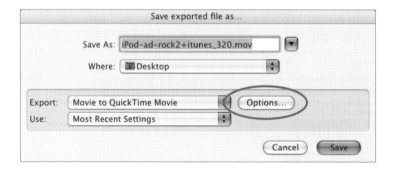

For this exercise, we're only interested in affecting the color in the video track of the movie. The settings for Sound and the options for Internet Streaming have no effect on the color in the movie.

5   In the Video area, click the Filter button.

6   In the Filter dialog that appears, toggle open the Adjustments triangle from the list in the upper-left corner of the dialog and select the ColorSync option.

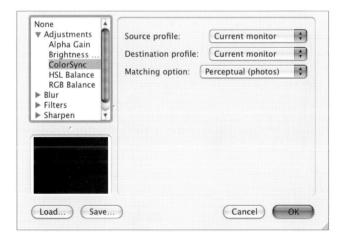

The ColorSync filter dialog lets you select source and destination profiles, as well as a matching option, or rendering intent.

7   Choose a source profile for your movie from the "Source profile" pop-up menu. For example, if you captured the video using a DV camera or exported the movie from iMovie or Final Cut Pro in the United States, then choose an NTSC profile. If you're working on video outside of the United States, choose a PAL/SECAM profile. If you you don't know the source profile, choose Current monitor.

NOTE ▶ NTSC and PAL profiles are installed with Adobe Photoshop and are available for download from the Adobe Web site.

8   Choose a destination profile for your movie from the "Destination profile" pop-up menu. For example, if you want to stream the movie over the Internet, select sRGB Profile to ensure that the colors in the movie are in gamut for most Web viewers.

9   Choose "Perceptual (photos)" from the "Matching option" pop-up menu. This is your rendering intent. Choosing "Perceptual (photos)" ensures that none of your color will be clipped when the movie is viewed. Clipped colors can appear as unattractive moving blotches.

The ColorSync filter dialog should now look like the following figure, including with a preview in the lower-left corner:

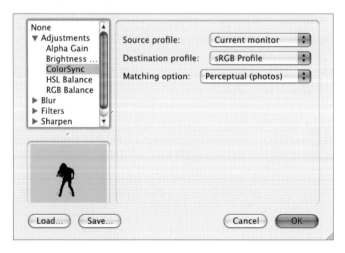

10 Click OK to close the ColorSync filter dialog and return to the Movie Settings dialog. Note that the ColorSync filter settings now appear in the dialog.

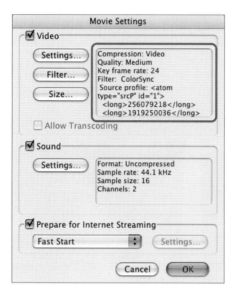

11 Click OK to close the Movie Settings dialog and return to the "Save exported file as" dialog.

12 Enter a filename for the new movie in the Save As text box and choose when you want to save it. Make sure Movie to QuickTime Move is chosen from the Export pop-up menu and that Most Recent Settings is chosen in the Use pop-up menu. Then click Save.

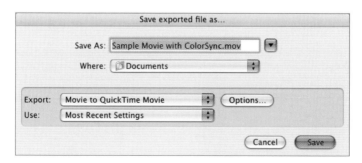

Depending on the size of the movie and the speed of your Mac, it may take some time to process the file. ColorSync matches each frame of video is from the source profile to the destination profile. When the file is saved, check out the difference between the original and the color-managed versions.

13 Press Command-O to open the original, un-color-managed video in QuickTime Player alongside the color-managed version. Play both files side by side, and compare the results. Depending on the profiles used, you may not see any differences.

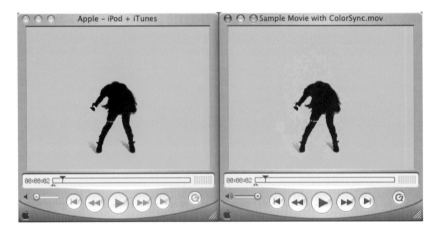

What You've Learned

- You can soft proof an image, illustration, or page layout to the Web by using the sRGB profile, and to video by using the NTSC or PAL profile.

- When preparing images for the Web or video, convert the color data from its working color space to the target color space, and embed the profile in the image file.

- Apple Safari and Microsoft Internet Explorer (version 5.5) both support ColorSync for displaying images with color management.

- QuickTime movies can be color managed between devices. For example, you can transform a movie to the sRGB color space in preparation for streaming over the Internet.

Apple's Digital Production Platform: An Integrated Workflow

Apple has developed a line of professional film, video, and audio production applications that, taken together, give professionals an affordable high-performance, integrated digital production platform. Each product is recognized as an industry standard in its respective field. When used together, they form a complete pipeline from content creation to delivery.

Here's a brief overview of how the four keystone applications—Final Cut Pro, Shake, Logic, and DVD Studio Pro—work together in a variety of standard production workflows.

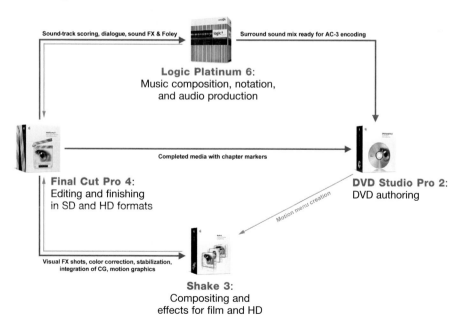

Sound-track scoring, dialogue, sound FX & Foley   Surround sound mix ready for AC-3 encoding

Logic Platinum 6:
Music composition, notation,
and audio production

Completed media with chapter markers

Final Cut Pro 4:
Editing and finishing
in SD and HD formats

DVD Studio Pro 2:
DVD authoring

Motion menu creation

Visual FX shots, color correction, stabilization,
integration of CG, motion graphics

Shake 3:
Compositing and
effects for film and HD

It's worth noting that because Apple takes a platform approach to its professional applications, the products also work well with complementary third-party solutions like Alias Wavefront's Maya, Adobe's After Effects and Photoshop, Avid's Media Composer, and Digidesign's ProTools.

Final Cut Pro

Final Cut Pro is a fully scalable nonlinear editing system designed to work with all standard video formats from DV to High Definition. More than just an editing application, Final Cut Pro lets you easily add filters and transitions to clips and play them in real time using an effects engine known as RT Extreme. Real-time color correction, customizable keyboard commands, dynamic and asymmetric trimming, broadcast video scopes, and support for multichannel audio editing, mixing, and output are a few of the features that make Final Cut Pro a great tool for serious editors. Four integrated applications are also included with Final Cut Pro:

LiveType is a powerful title generation tool that lets you quickly and easily integrate dynamic, animated titles, objects, and textures into your video content. All elements are fully rendered 32-bit animations, which can be scaled from DV to Film Academy formats.

Soundtrack is an audio content-creation application that lets you build original, high-quality musical scores for your video. It uses royalty-free *loops* as the building blocks for musical compositions, and includes thousands of loops and sound effects that can easily be arranged to pre-defined markers in Final Cut Pro.

Cinema Tools is a sophisticated relational database designed to track the relationship between original film negatives and their digitized media counterparts. It gives editors and filmmakers the ability to shoot and finish on film and 24P (HD) while using Final Cut Pro for their editing.

Compressor is a high-speed encoding application that gives you an efficient way to convert video and audio content for a variety of distribution formats. Completed Final Cut Pro sequences are exported to Compressor and encoded to MPEG-4, MPEG-2, and other standard formats for distribution on the Web, CD, or DVD.

In the Pipeline

For more robust compositing, special-effects plates can be exported from Final Cut Pro and layered and manipulated in Shake. Audio elements in need of additional processing and mixing can be exported to Logic Audio for sweetening, and rough scores created in Soundtrack can be enhanced by professional composers in Logic. When completed, all treated media can be imported to DVD Studio Pro for professional DVD authoring.

Shake

Shake is a high-end compositing system used to create visual effects for award-winning broadcast commercials and box-office–champion feature films like *The Lord of the Rings* and *The Matrix*. Unlike the timeline-based compositing in Final Cut Pro, Shake uses a node-based architecture. Each operator is a discrete unit that can be plugged into other operators in an incredibly flexible, nonlinear fashion, creating a detailed process tree that leads to the final composited shot.

Like Final Cut Pro, Shake is resolution independent, so it can handle all standard video and film formats. Shake also includes two industry-standard keyers for greenscreen and bluescreen work: Photron's Primatte and Framestore/CFC's Keylight.

Shake is typically used for combining elements from multiple sources into a single image, creating the illusion that everything was filmed "in camera." These elements typically include 3D animation, particles, procedural painting, and live-action plates. Shake's compositing capabilities are complemented by an abundance of color correctors, necessary tools for the professional compositing artist.

One of Shake's greatest strengths is its customization. Almost every parameter in Shake can be linked to another via simple expressions, so it's easy to blur a light source as it gets brighter, or make an airplane fade into the sky as it shrinks toward the horizon. The MacroMaker lets you easily create custom plug-ins. A generous community of Shake users means that dozens of free plug-ins are available for download from www.highend2d.com.

In the Pipeline

In general, any shot that requires multilayered visual effects can be composited with more ease and precision in Shake than in Final Cut Pro. One of the most common shots to be sent to Shake is a bluescreen or greenscreen. While Final Cut Pro has built-in keyers, Shake includes far more sophisticated keying techniques based on color difference and 3D color space technology. Foreground and background contrast and color can be matched, background lighting can be wrapped around the foreground image, and problem edges can be isolated and treated.

Another common use for Shake is footage stabilization and match moving. Shake can stabilize position, scale, rotation, and perspective, salvaging shaky footage that would otherwise be unusable. Using the same technology, Shake can match the motion in a camera shot so that composited elements seem to "belong" in the scene.

Logic

Logic Platinum is a complete virtual recording studio used to create and edit music sound tracks, dialogue, and sound effects as well as to mix and master final audio files (including surround sound). Logic contains a fully scalable mixing console, dozens of effects processors, and the option to add Emagic's world-class software-based synthesizers as virtual instruments. In addition, it is designed with advanced MIDI handling to access external synthesizers, keyboards, and other MIDI-enabled instruments. The software contained in Logic rivals some of the most sophisticated hardware-based recording studios in the world in both audio quality and creative control.

Audio is either imported into Logic in the form of a digital audio file or acquired live by arming an audio track and recording. Once the media is acquired, it can be positioned in a musical timeline, and its pitch and tempo can be modified to match the primary key and tempo of the composition. Typically, levels are then set and automated (for example, fading the electric guitar solo up and down at the appropriate times), effects such as reverb and delay are added, and the final mix is prepared either as a stereo file or a surround sound mix.

Logic works simultaneously with SMPTE timecode, meaning that sounds can be positioned based on events in time, rather than on musical beats and bars. This makes it ideal for work on film and video sound tracks. Video can be previewed in a floating window or viewed as a thumbnail track in order to make precise matches to cuts and significant events in the narrative.

In the Pipeline

There are several ways in which Logic can be used in a film and video production pipeline. The most obvious is in the creation of a musical score. Final Cut Pro's Soundtrack is a great way to quickly create custom royalty-free music, but it can only match the action and dynamics of your visuals to a point. To really finesse the sound track and create a sound bed that includes unique composition and performance by professional musicians, the sound track will need to be ported into Logic.

Logic is also indispensable for working with nonmusical elements in a project. Dialogue in a sound track often needs to be compressed to allow audiences to hear an actor's whispers. Bad pronunciation that could ruin an otherwise great take can be cleaned up by copying and merging consonant and vowel sounds from elsewhere in the audio track. Room ambience can be restored in scenes where overdubbed dialogue had replaced the original audio.

One of the most exciting uses for Logic is the addition of Foley and sound effects, which tend to make or break the professional polish of many movies. Not only does Logic enable you to place and manipulate effects from sound-effects libraries and Foley recording sources, but the virtual-instrument options mean that entirely new sounds can be generated for unique applications: the deep rumble of an earthquake or the throaty whine of a futuristic jet car.

Surround sound mixing is directly incorporated into Logic. Music, dialogue, and effects can all be positioned in a virtual audio plane and animate across that plane relative to onscreen action. So helicopters flying from behind the camera to the front can be accompanied by the noise of their blades starting in the rear speakers of a surround sound system, then moving to the front. DVD Studio Pro includes a Dolby AC3 surround sound encoding system, which can take the Logic output tracks and encode them for distribution via DVD.

Finally, one often-overlooked but significant role for Logic is audio mastering. Sound tracks that sound spectacular on the monitor speakers in an editing suite can sound muddy and distorted when played back on a home stereo or the tinny speakers that accompany most television sets. Logic comes with high-quality audio mastering tools to tame the dynamic range of a sound track so that it is compatible with a wide range of listening environments.

DVD Studio Pro

DVD Studio Pro is a complete DVD authoring platform. It takes video, audio, and image content and combines them into an interactive menu-driven DVD. This can include motion menus, chapter and title access, special features, slide shows, and more. Basically, anything you've seen in a commercial DVD product can be created using DVD Studio Pro.

DVD Studio Pro uses a new intuitive project interface to combine different menus and media into a completed interactive piece. Authored works are designed to meet international DVD specifications, making them compatible with all compliant DVD playback units on the market. With a SuperDrive, finished projects can be burned directly to DVD-R for immediate test and playback. For larger production runs, the project can be mastered to DLT (tape) and sent to a duplication facility.

The application also includes Compressor, a powerful software-based MPEG2 encoding tool, as well as the AC3 encoder mentioned in the Logic section above. In essence, Compressor uses two-pass variable bit-rate encoding to read through the video file, analyze what changed between frames, and then store only the changed information. Using this analysis data, Compressor can encode the footage with a higher data rate for scenes that need it and a lower one for those that don't. The result is extremely high quality MPEG2 video that meets or exceeds the quality of real-time PCI-based professional encoders.

In the Pipeline

DVD Studio Pro is obviously the last step in a production workflow, where media content is assembled for delivery. The DVD authoring may be one of several delivery streams coming from the Final Cut Pro media; others may include video mastering, Web streaming, or even external film edits. One handy feature of Final Cut Pro is its ability to create and export chapter markers for use in DVD Studio Pro.

Other ways DVD Studio Pro and Final Cut Pro can work together include the creation of 4:3 pan-and-scan versions of a 16:9 piece, preparation of multiple-angle clips, and development of complex motion menus. Shake can be used for motion menus, its nonlinear workflow making it ideal for quickly generating alternate motion selection and rollover button states.

Glossary

absolute colorimetric A rendering intent that leaves in-gamut colors
unchanged and effectively clips the colors that fall out of that gamut. This
rendering is based on the source's white point and is suitable for proofing to
simulate the output of a particular device.

Adobe RGB (1998) A common working-space profile that provides the best
option for a print-production color workflow, both for desktop photo printers
and printing presses.

API (application programming interface) An interface that allows software
developers to use the capabilities of a color management system. APIs contain
code that can be used as part of another application.

black point compensation In Adobe Photoshop, the setting that maps the
darkest black in the source profile to the darkest black of the destination profile and adjusts the other values accordingly.

calibration Changing a device to a standard or to a known state by adjusting
tonal curves.

CIE (Commission Internationale d'Eclairage) The International
Commission on Illlumination. A color standards organization.

CMM (color management module) Also called the *color matching method.*
A software algorithm that converts colors between profiles. Specifically, the CMM
translates data from one device's colors to another via a device-independent
color space. When a color is in gamut for one device but not another, the CMM
must select the next closest reproducible color. This is called *gamut mapping.*
The ICC profile specification supports four gamut-mapping options, called
rendering intents.

CMS (color management system) An organized way of controlling color reproduction between devices, software, and the user. Color management interprets the reproduction of color from one device to another to ensure that the intent is accurately communicated.

CMYK A working space for four-color process printing made of ink-and-paper combinations, dot-gain settings, and separation options such as ink limits. Printing presses are CMYK.

colorimeter An instrument that measures the color value of a sample, using color filters. A colorimeter can determine if two colors are the same, but it does not take into account the light under which a sample is measured. Colorimeters are often used to calibrate displays.

color mode A way of describing all colors according to specific definitions. The RGB color mode, for example, represents each color as a mixture of red, green, and blue. Other common color modes are CIE Lab, CMYK, and HSB.

color space A model that represents part of the visible spectrum. Color from one device is mapped from the device-specific value to a device-independent value in a color space. Once in an independent space, the color can be mapped to another device-specific space.

ColorSync A color management system that has been part of the Mac operating system for about 10 years. In Mac OS X, ColorSync is thoroughly integrated with the entire operating system and is available to all native Mac OS X applications.

ColorSync Utility The ColorSync Utility is a centralized application for setting preferences, viewing installed profiles, assigning profiles to devices, and repairing profiles that do not conform to the current ICC specification.

contract proof A printer's proof that serves as the agreed-upon standard to be matched by the press run.

D50, D65 See *white point.*

densitometer An instrument that measures the density of ink on paper (that is, the absorption of light), not color values.

destination profile The working-space profile that defines the results of a color conversion from a source profile.

device characterization The process of making device profiles. Color values from the device are measured with a dedicated instrument such as a colorimeter. Then, specialized software compares the measured values to the known values of those colors, and it uses the differences to generate a profile. The idea is to measure a wide range of colors so that the software can determine the gamut of the device.

device dependent Describes color values that are contingent upon a particular device's reproduction characteristics.

device independent Said of a color space whose color definitions remain the same, regardless of the capabilities of any specific device. In 1931, the CIE (Commission Internationale de l'Eclairage) established standards for a series of color spaces that represent the visible spectrum. These color spaces form the foundation of device-independent color for color management.

device profile See *profile.*

display A computer monitor.

drift The change over time in the color output of a device such as a printer as the device ages or the manufacturer changes the inks or paper.

embedded profile A source profile saved in a document. Embedded profiles are supported in the Photoshop PSD, EPS, and PDF file formats as well as in TIFF, JPEG, and PICT files.

G

gamma The contrast of midtones displayed on a monitor. The higher the number, the greater the contrast. The Mac Standard gamma is 1.8; the PC Standard is 2.2.

gamut The range of colors reproducible by a device such as a display, scanner, printer, or press. Each device has a unique gamut that is dictated by its characteristics—the types of inks it uses to print, the type of technology it uses to capture images, and so on.

gamut mapping Bringing colors that are out of gamut for a device to their nearest in-gamut equivalents.

I

ICC (International Color Consortium) An organization that establishes color-management standards, the first of which was the ICC profile. ICC profiles are supported by virtually all vendors of color-imaging hardware and software.

IT8 A common target used in profiling scanners and printers: IT8.7/1 is for transmissive media (transparencies or film), IT8.7/2 for reflective media (prints).

L

Lab plot A visual three-dimensional representation of the CIE Lab color space.

P

perceptual A rendering intent that works to preserve the visual relationship between colors so that they are perceived as natural to the human eye, even if the colors themselves actually change. This rendering intent is suitable for photographic images.

profile A compilation of data on a specific device's color information, including its gamut, color space, and modes of operation. A profile represents a device's color-reproduction capabilities—and is essential to making the color management system work.

RAW A file format that contains unmodified data captured by a digital camera.

R

relative colorimetric A rendering intent suitable for photographic images. It compares the highlight of the source color space to that of the destination color space and shifts out-of-gamut colors to the closest reproducible color in the destination color space.

rendering intent The method by which colors that are out of gamut for a selected output device are mapped to that device's reproducible gamut.

RGB A working space whose colors are defined by their levels of red, green, and blue. It is the color space for displays, cameras, scanners, and some desktop printers.

RIP (raster image processor) A specialized printer driver that replaces the driver that comes with your printer. It takes input from applications and converts, or rasterizes, the information into data that the printer understands so that it can put dots on a page. Software RIPs typically offer features not found in standard printer drivers.

saturation intent A rendering intent suitable for business graphs or charts in which bright, saturated colors are more important than the exact relationship between colors. Saturation is the degree to which a color appears to be pure, without gray.

S

soft proof The onscreen simulation by a display of the output from printer or press.

source profile The profile of a file before it undergoes color conversion.

spectrophotometer An instrument that measures the wavelength of color across an entire spectrum of colors. As it can be used to profile both displays and printers, the spectrophotometer is preferred for device profiling.

sRGB A common working space designed to represent the average PC monitor. Because of its small gamut, it is suitable for Web graphics but not for print production.

SWOP An acronym for *specifications for web offset publications,* a standard printing-press profile. *Web* here refers to a web press, not the Internet.

T

tagged Refers to an image that has been saved in a working-space profile.

target A reference file used to profile a device such as a scanner or digital camera. It often contains patches whose color values have been measured. The output from a device is then compared with the target.

TWAIN A standard interface for scanner hardware and driver.

U

untagged Refers to a document or an image that lacks an embedded profile.

W

white point The color temperature of a display, measured in kelvins. The higher the white point, the bluer the white; the lower the white point, the redder. The native white point for the Mac is D50 (5000 kelvins); for Windows, it is D65 (6500 kelvins).

working space The color space in which you edit a file. It can be different from the original color space of the file, which is called the *document* color space. Working spaces are based either on color-space profiles such as Adobe RGB or on device profiles.

Index

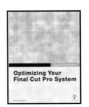